FOCUS ON

Advanced English C.A.E.

GRAMMAR PRACTICE

REVISED AND UPDATED

Longman

RICHARD WALTON
SERIES EDITOR: Sue O'Connell

Pearson Education Limited
Edinburgh Gate
Harlow
Essex CM20 2JE
England
and Associated Companies throughout the world

www.longman.com

First published by Thomas Nelson and Sons Ltd 1994
This edition published by Pearson Education Ltd, 1999
Thirteenth impression 2008

ISBN-13: 978-0-58232571-5

Set in 11/13.5 Minion

Printed in Spain by Graficas Estella

Author's acknowledgement
Many thanks to Sue O'Connell for keeping the book 'focused' and staying positive: and to Roberta for putting up with it all.

I would also like to thank the students and staff of St Clare's, Oxford for their help in piloting the material and for their support.

The publishers are grateful to the following for permission to reproduce copyright material: Philip Allan Publishers Ltd for an adapted extract from 'Special Agents' by Andrew Jones in SOCIOLOGY REVIEW vol. 7 No 1, September 1977 and an extract from 'Thinking about family life' by David Morgan in SOCIOLOGY REVIEW vol. 7 No 4, 1998; British Airways for an extract from an article by David Hewson in BRITISH AIRWAYS BUSINESS LIFE July/August 1998; BBC WILDLIFE MAGAZINE on behalf of the authors, for extracts from 'Mystery of the dying frogs' by Tim Halliday & 'Small is beautiful' by Jonathan Porritt in BBC WILDLIFE MAGAZINE October 1997 p29 & pp21–22; Brockman Inc. on behalf of the author, for an extract from THE RISE AND FALL OF THE THIRD CHIMPANZEE by Jared Diamond; Guardian Newspapers Ltd for a slightly adapted extract from 'Office Politics' by Guy Browning in THE GUARDIAN WEEKEND 6.6.98; Guild of Master Craftsman Publications Ltd for and advertisement for a desk editor in THE INDEPENDENT 13.10.93; Penguin Books Ltd for an adapted extract from BETTER READER, FASTER READER by Manya and Eric De Leeuw (Pelican Original) Copyright © Manya and Eric De Leeuw, 1965.

We have been unable to trace the copyright holder of the letter 'Pick Strawberry Fields for the heritage beat' from Mr Gerald Murphy to THE INDEPENDENT and would appreciate any information which would enable us to do so.

Illustrations by Nigel Paige, Anne Burchell
Designed by Annette Peppis
Project Managed by Dave Francis

Contents

1 Use Your Head   4

Dictionary skills – Abbreviations; parts of
speech; tenses; dependent prepositions
Grammar – Conditionals 0, 1, 2; *despite/in
spite of*; *although/but*
Phrasal verbs – Word order
Phrasal verbs – Can you split it up?
Prefixes – *under* and *over*
Writing – Informal letter
Word formation
Wordcheck – Collocations
Error correction

2 Severe Weather   11

Vocabulary – Collocations; Idioms and
metaphors
Contrast links
Collocations
Prepositions
Writing – Formal letter
Spelling – That can't be right!
Grammar – Review of passives and causative
have/get something done; passives for formal
effect
Dependent prepositions
Wordcheck – Weather

3 Time Eaters   16

Vocabulary – Register and style
no matter …
Grammar – *will* vs *going to*; future time
clauses; guess the ending; present tenses,
modal verbs

4 Stress   20

Cause and effect
Grammar – *-ing* forms; prepositions and
conjunctions + *-ing*; *-ing* or infinitive?; *-ing*
nouns; *-ing* adjectives
Word building – Verb formation
Dependent prepositions
Collocations
Wordcheck – Stress and relaxation

Progress Test One   25

5 Globe Trotting   29

Cohesive devices
Grammar – Past simple vs past continuous;
past perfect simple and continuous
Phrasal verbs – Phrasal verbs with *up*; in
other words; three-word phrasal verbs
Reference links
Word stress – Air travel
Writing – Formal letter
Editing for phrasal verbs
Wordcheck – Collocations

6 Language Matters   35

Relative clauses – Relative pronouns; different
endings; reduced relative clauses; fill in the gaps
like, as and *alike*
Comparison – Comparatives and
superlatives, as … as, complete the sentences
Degrees of comparison
Linking and logical devices – addition,
concession, contrast
Spelling
Emphasisers
Review writing

7 The Ages of Man   41

Grammar – *used to …* vs *be/get used to …*;
past simple or present perfect; present perfect
simple and continuous; stative vs dynamic
verbs
Dictionary skills – Connotation; parts of
speech; metaphors and idioms; collocation;
word formation (derivations); register;
pronunciation and stress
Reported speech
Expressions with *make*
Discourse cloze
Wordcheck – Age

8 Personally Speaking   46

Compound adjectives of character
The … the … – comparatives
Phrasal verbs
Grammar – The passive; fill in the gaps;
make/cause, etc.
Writing – Informal letter
Wordcheck – Character and personality
Lexical cloze

Progress Test Two   50

9 Mind Your Manners   55

Inversion after negative introductions
Modal verbs
Collocations – verb + noun; verb + adverb;
adjective + noun
Dictionary skills – Opposites – prefixes;
synonyms and antonyms; phonetics; spelling
vs pronunciation; pronunciation
Type 3 and mixed conditionals
Writing – Report writing
Register cloze

10 State of the Union   61

Grammar – Review of *-ing* forms and
infinitives; cleft sentences and introductory *it*
Collocations with *do/make/have/get*
Phrasal verbs
Dependent prepositions
Writing – Information sheet
Structural cloze
Word formation
Wordcheck – Relationships

11 Last Chance to See

Relative clauses – Punctuation; relative
clauses with prepositions
Phrasal verbs – Tense and structure; different
meanings
Expressing the future
Quantifiers – *each/every*, *either/neither*
Linking and logical devices – cause and
result, purpose and time
Discourse cloze
Writing – Formal letter
Wordcheck – The environment

Progress Test Three   71

12 Living Dangerously   75

Collocations and idioms
Emphatic structures
Phrasal verbs – Tense and structure; different
meanings
Past tenses
Conditionals – Conditional 3; 1st, 2nd, 3rd
and mixed conditionals
Dependent prepositions
Writing – Article
Structural cloze
Wordcheck – Fire

13 Mind and Body   80

Pronouns – object, reflexive and reciprocal
Past tenses for hypothetical situations
Vocabulary – Word building; adjectives
Phrasal verbs
Dictionary skills – Collocations; metaphors
and idioms
Expressions of concession
Writing – Character reference
Word formation

14 Testing Times   86

Review of grammatical and syntactical
structures – Tense forms and time;
conditionals; structures after verbs;
modals/modal perfects; passives; linkers;
participle clauses; emphatic structures
-ing forms – *-ing* or infinitive?; *-ing* forms,
infinitive with or without *to*
Tenses
Review of tenses
Writing – Report
Wordcheck – Studying and examinations
Editing skills

Progress Test Four   93

Answer Key   98

SB = Student's Book

1 ▶ Use Your Head

1 Dictionary skills

1.1 Abbreviations

Give two examples for each of the following dictionary abbreviations. The first one has been done for you.

1 PREP *with, from*
2 ADV ....
3 SING ....
4 CONJ ....
5 PRON ....
6 N [U] or UNCOUNT ....
7 PL ....
8 ADJ ....
9 V ....
10 PASS ....

STUDY TIP   Using a dictionary

▶ As an advanced learner, you will find a good monolingual dictionary an essential tool. Apart from spelling and meanings, a dictionary can tell you:
– part of speech
– pronunciation – if you can recognise phonetic script
– word stress – /rɪˈtɜːn/ or /rɪtɜːn/
– word formation
– collocations
– useful phrases the word is used in

1.2 Parts of speech

Decide the grammatical function of the word *fast* in each of the sentences below. Use your dictionary to check your answers.

1 If you take the fast train, you should be there in under an hour.
2 Many religions require their followers to fast at certain times of the year.
3 The car got stuck fast in the wet sand so we just left it there.
4 When it started raining, we all ran inside as fast as we could.
5 Some prisoners began a fast to protest against the appalling conditions.
6 By the time I got home, the children were already fast asleep.

1.3 Tenses

Complete the following sentences with the correct form of the verbs in brackets. Then fill in the name of the tense you have used. See the example.

1 Dan *hates* doing the washing-up. (hate – *present simple*)
2 Hi, Laura. Long time no see. How .... it .... ? (go – ....)
3 Sorry to keep you. How long .... you .... ? (wait – ....)
4 I sincerely hope they .... the building work by the end of next month. (finish – ....)
5 What .... you .... between 5 and 6pm last Saturday? (do – ....)
6 Good news everybody! We .... to build a new gymnasium with the new government grant. (can – ....)
7 .... Julia ever .... seriously ill before her trip to India last year? (be – ....)
8 Just think, this time next month I .... here for ten years! (work – ....)
9 Does anyone want a sandwich? No thanks, I .... just .... lunch. (have – ....)
10 Where on earth .... you .... those shoes? They're awful! (buy – ....)
11 I hope I .... on a sun-drenched beach in Italy this time tomorrow. (sit – ....)
12 We .... through the forest for two or three hours when we realised we were lost! (walk – ....)

1.4 Dependent prepositions

Complete the following sentences by putting the correct preposition in the space provided. The first one has been done for you.

1 Moral and social responsibility should be integrated *into* every child's schooling.
2 It's impossible to attend .... a task properly if you're worrying .... something else.
3 Kelly has great confidence .... her children's abilities.
4 It's a good idea to make notes .... what you're reading if you want to remember it.
5 Unfortunately, many university courses do not provide students .... the basic study skills they really need.

6 Jack took early retirement as he was losing his grip
   .... the job.

7 Apparently, an interest in reading in later life is
   closely related .... how much your parents
   read to you as a child.

8 Ron usually primes himself .... plenty of
   black coffee before starting the night shift.

9 I find it very hard to commit historical dates
   .... memory.

10 Lack of sleep can seriously interfere .... your
   ability to think rationally.

2 Grammar

2.1 Conditionals 0, 1 and 2 ▶ Focus on Grammar, SB page 14

Complete the following conditional sentences with
suitable phrases. Look at the example given.

1 OK, OK, I'll lend you the money as long as you *pay
  me back* next week.

2 What would you do if your car .... miles
  from anywhere?

3 If you .... woollen clothes in hot water,
  they shrink.

4 Quite frankly, I think you're going to fail the exam
  unless .... harder.

5 I know he's hardly ever around these days but if you
  .... , tell him to get back in touch.

6 But supposing our train is late, how ....
  the airport on time?

7 I can't get off to sleep at night unless .... a
  hot drink.

8 If my boyfriend spoke to me like that, ...
  his face.

9 You can borrow my video camera on condition that
  .... properly.

10 If you drop a cat, it always .... on its feet.

11 I'd apply for that job as an interpreter if
   .... better Russian.

12 Should .... further information, please
   contact our publicity officer.

13 I'm going to take a big pullover in case ....
   very cold.

14 I'm sure you .... those headaches all the
   time if you wore your glasses more often.

15 Provided .... no more objections, we'll
   continue with the next point on the agenda.

16 Suppose .... on a desert island, how would
   you survive?

17 I'd go and see the doctor with that rash if
   .... you.

18 We should be able to play tennis on Friday afternoon
   unless .... , of course.

19 Should .... in the neighbourhood, feel free
   to call in.

20 I'd play a lot more sport if I .... so much
   work to do.

STUDY TIP Conditionals

▶ Although you cannot use *'ll* after *if* in most
conditional sentences, there is one time when you can.
This is to express willingness or volition:
e.g. If you'll clear the table, I'll wash the dishes.

2.2 *despite/in spite of; although/but* ▶ Study Box, SB page 17

Match the first half of the sentences in Column A with
their endings in Column B then add an appropriate linking
word or phrase. The first one has been done for you.

A

1 Joan is very hard-working   ☑ D

2 .... Lucy lived in Mexico for three years, ☐

3 Joe's parents wanted him to be a doctor ☐

4 .... teachers can help students learn, ☐

5 .... what you might have heard, ☐

6 Sue passed all of her exams

7 .... they lived almost opposite the
  state school ☐

8 .... of drinking six cups of strong, black
  coffee ☐

9 We made ourselves understood ☐

10 .... all the special offers ☐

B

A .... not doing any revision at all.

B .... of not speaking any Greek.

C Jack and Ruth sent their daughter to a private place
  ten miles away.

D *but* she's not very imaginative.

E I refused to buy any encyclopaedias.

F she only speaks a few words of Spanish.

G I just couldn't stay awake.

H students must learn for themselves.

I .... he wanted to learn to write plays.

J there is no quick and easy way to learn a language.

3 Phrasal verbs

3.1 Word order

In some, but not all, of the sentences below the word order of the phrasal verbs and objects is wrong. Make any corrections that you think are necessary. See the example given.

1   If there are any words you don't understand, look
    ▼up (them) in your dictionaries.
2   Quick, I haven't got a pen. Can you jot Jack's phone number down for me?
3   You don't have to give me an answer right away. Think over it and let me know tomorrow.
4   'Are you going to the party next Friday?'
    'Yes, I'm really looking forward to it.'
5   Could you look this article through and tell me what you think of it?
6   'I don't think we'll be able to play the match in all this rain.'
    'No, let's put off it until tomorrow.'
7   'Mrs McCarthy, I've got your husband on the line.'
    'OK. Put him through.'
8   It was such a good book I just couldn't put down it.
9   Harry's family always believed in his innocence and stood by him throughout the murder trial.
10 'I see you're still smoking, Chris.'
    'Yes, but I'm really trying to give up it.'

3.2 Can you split it up? ▶ Focus on Grammar, SB page 19

In the following sentences add a particle to complete the phrasal verb and an appropriate object pronoun (*it, me, them*, etc) in the CORRECT place – either before or after the particle. See the example provided.

1   OK, you read out the phone numbers and I'll jot
    them down.
2   Where's the remote control?
    I don't know. I was just looking ....
    ....
3   That cheese in the fridge had gone off so I threw
    ....

4   He doesn't look like his father much but he takes
    .... in the way he behaves.
5   Their company has gone bankrupt and they only set
    .... two years ago!
6   Look, don't keep complaining to me about it. If your steak is underdone, send ....!
7   'Did you believe that story about a long-lost brother?'
    'No, not a word of it. I'm sure she was making
    .... '
8   'What did little Patrick think of his first visit to the swimming pool?'
    'Oh, he took .... like a duck to water!'
9   You don't have to give me an answer right now.
    Think .... for a while.
10 The form was so complicated that she had to ask her accountant to fill .... for her.
11 I've been given this algebra problem to solve before tomorrow morning and I just can't work
    ....
12 His wife left him for another man and he's never really got ....
13 I still don't understand this word and I've just looked .... in the dictionary!
14 As they didn't have anywhere to stay, we put
    .... for the night.
15 Nina fainted in the heat and we had to bring
    .... with smelling salts.

4 Prefixes – *under* and *over*

▶ Word formation, SB page 20

4.1 Fill in the spaces below with words beginning with *under* and their opposites. Look at the example provided.

1 smaller than average or normal (adj)
2 fail to guess or understand the real cost, size or difficulty of something (v)
3 not express an idea fully or adequately (v)
4 weak and unhealthy due to lack of food (adj)
5 charge too little money for something (v)
6 having too few people for the amount of work (adj)
7 not cooked for long enough (adj)
8 wearing clothes that are not attractive or formal enough for an event (adj)
9 make too little use of something (v)
10 lacking the money, education, possessions and opportunities that the average person has (adj)
11 fail to appreciate how skilful, important someone or something is (v)
12 give too little light to a piece of photographic film (v)

	Word	Opposite
1	undersized	oversized
2		
3		
4		
5		
6		
7		
8		
9		
10		
11		
12		

4.2 Now complete these sentences using any of the words from 4.1. See the example provided.

1 There was far too much light and all my photos were *overexposed.*
2 Don't you think you're a bit .... for a barbecue in that suit?
3 The baby was a bit .... at birth but she's put on weight well.
4 Calling his behaviour criminal is rather an .... It was just a mistake.
5 I think 45 minutes is an .... of the time it will take. I'd allow an hour.
6 The office is .... so some people will have to be made redundant.
7 The council is trying to promote the new sports facilities, which are .... at present.
8 I'm hopeless at preparing pasta. I always .... how much to cook and we end up either eating it for three days or throwing it away.
9 I can't stand meat that is so .... that it has blood oozing out of it.
10 I find his songs very repetitive. I think he's really .... as a singer, to be honest.
11 To say we were surprised by the news of his arrest would be an ....
12 Many of the children were clearly .... and suffering from various diseases.
13 It's a very good restaurant. But be warned, they tend to ....
14 Although she came from an .... family background, she went on to become one of the most highly paid lawyers in Britain.

5 Writing – Informal letter

In the following letter, there are 7 mistakes of layout and style. One has been marked for you. There are also 7 missing phrases. Find the other 6 mistakes and complete the 7 missing phrases.

Andy Kulbacher
Bramley Road (25)
Burnville BV2 6BZ

23rd Oct, 20—

Dear friend,

it was very nice to (1) .... after such a long time. (2) .... to hear that you've settled down in your new job in Valencia and are getting into the local way of life!

As you know, I'm still working at the same language school as before although now I'm in charge of marketing our courses in Europe! So it's a lot more responsibility and lots of travelling. As it happens, I'm coming to Valencia next month and (3) .... favour! I desperately need the names, addresses and phone numbers of the directors of all the local English language schools and I can't seem to get that sort of information in this country.

(4) .... if you could go through all the local yellow pages and send me information. Please don't

(5) .... if you can't manage it, I can always do it when I get there.

(6) .... , we must definitely meet up when I'm over. (7) .... see you soon.

Looking forward to hearing from you. Yours sincerely,

Andy

6 Word formation

6.1 Complete the following grid, paying particular attention to whether the required word is grammatically positive (+) or negative (–). See the examples provided.

1	efficient (adj +)	*efficiency* (noun +)
2	respond (verb +)	*irresponsible* (adj –)
3	benefit (noun +)	.... (adj +)
4	complex (adj +)	.... (noun +)
5	intellect (noun +)	.... (adj +)
6	conceive (verb +)	.... (noun –)
7	deceive (verb +)	.... (adj +)
8	anxious (adj +)	.... (noun +)
9	honesty (noun +)	.... (adj –)
10	explain (verb +)	.... (noun +)
11	photograph (noun +)	.... (adj +)
12	attend (verb +)	.... (adj –)
13	psychology (noun +)	.... (adj +)
14	invest (verb +)	.... (noun +)
15	appear (verb +)	.... (noun –)

6.2 Now complete the following sentences with suitable words from the exercise above.

16 A 'cheat' is someone who behaves in a .... and .... way.

17 There is a popular .... that all British people are monarchists. This is simply not true!

18 Sara refused to provide the police with any .... for the .... of such a large sum of money.

19 The .... effects of taking regular exercise are both physical and ....

20 Children often feel a great deal of .... about their first day at school.

21 Although Rita was often .... in class, she had a virtually .... memory and got top grades in all her exams.

22 The .... of her arguments left us all in a state of confusion.

23 I like to relax with a good detective story – nothing too demanding or ....

24 The .... of our memories does not necessarily deteriorate with age.

7 Wordcheck – Collocations

Complete the sentences below by adding the correct verbs in the most suitable form from the box. The first one has been done for you.

parrot	report	undergo
circulate	assimilate	set yourself
produce	offer	chew over
~~consult~~	jot down	prove

1 If you don't know where it is, try *consulting* an atlas.

2 It's hard to .... information when feeling anxious.

3 Several students volunteered to .... psychological tests.

4 Details of the new grant were .... in the last edition of the college magazine.

5 Don't even try and write everything. Just .... the main points.

6 It's important to .... clear targets in your study programme.

7 Don't make the mistake of simply .... someone else's words when writing your own notes.

8 The teacher said mnemonics can help you memorise things and to .... the point he memorised various phrases the students came up with in other languages.

9 The headteacher could .... no explanation for such poor examination results.

10 I find it helpful to listen to classical music when I'm .... a problem.

11 So-called 'sleep learning' has failed to .... any beneficial effects to the learning process.

12 The findings of the tests were .... in the journal 'Psychobabble'.

8 Error correction

8.1 Parts of speech

<u>Underline</u> the unnecessary words in each of the following sentences and identify which part of speech it is. See the example given.

1 Remind me to telephone <u>to</u> my sister before the end of the day.   *preposition*
2 We really need an information about flights to Skopje.   ....
3 The modern life is complicated enough without more rules
   and regulations.   ....
4 They hope to can arrive before the start of the conference.   ....
5 Hadn't she been suggested creating two part-time jobs?   ....
6 If you don't know the answer, why don't you ask to the teacher?   ....
7 Prague which is a city I've always wanted to visit.   ....
8 Paul was in the hospital for three months after the accident.   ....
9 The shark which pushed silently through the seaweed and
   attacked the unsuspecting swimmers.   ....
10 There was an ominous silence as they entered into the room.   ....

8.2 Error correction

In most lines of the following text there is one unnecessary word. It is either grammatically incorrect or it does not fit in with the sense of the text. For each numbered line, find the unnecessary word and then write it in the space provided. Some lines are correct. Indicate these with a tick (✓). The first two lines have been done for you.

Mapping the mind's word processor

An area is deep in the left frontal half of the brain used to
process language has been pinpointed by a new brain-imager.
Dr Julie Fiez, who first reported the work, believes brain-imagers
will one day help to show that the causes of problems like dyslexia
and determine strategies to overcome language in difficulties.
The new imaging technique shows that the parts of the brain which
are 'working harder' because of blood flow has increased.
When some people being studied were asked to lift their left index
finger when they have heard a specific tone, word, syllable
or vowel. Others were asked only to listen without doing anything.
The brain's left frontal region was seen to be used only
when subjects had to show they had heard of the specific sound,
rather than just listened. Many regions are involved in listening
but this one appears to be involved when parts of a sound have to
be analysed to make up a decision, for instance how to correctly
pronounce the words 'lead' and 'tears' in the different contexts.

0	*is*
0	✓
1	....
2	....
3	....
4	....
5	....
6	....
7	....
8	....
9	....
10	....
11	....
12	....
13	....
14	....

2 ► # Severe Weather

1 Vocabulary

1.1 Collocations

Match each word in Column A with its partner in
Column B. See the example.

	A			B	
1	high	E	A	situation
2	gusty	☐	B	range
3	torrential	☐	C	warning
4	severe	☐	D	level
5	slight	☐	E	tides
6	desperate	☐	F	weather
7	flood	☐	G	seas
8	choppy	☐	H	rain
9	temperature	☐	I	winds
10	sea	☐	J	breeze

1.2 Idioms and metaphors

Complete the following sentences to make a suitable
common idiom or metaphor connected with the weather.

1 I'm really sorry I won't be able to see you this week
   but I'm absolutely *snowed* under with work.
2 'What's the capital of Peru?'
   'Sorry, I haven't got the .... idea!'
3 Jane and Steve have what you might call a
   .... relationship – they're always arguing
   and then making up again!
4 Julie is amazingly cheerful, she always greets
   everyone with a .... smile.
5 The decision to build the new motorway through
   the forest was met by .... of protest from
   local residents.
6 Tom has been .... Maria with presents to
   make up for forgetting their wedding anniversary
   last month.
7 One of the TV cameramen was hit in the leg when
   they were caught in a .... of bullets outside
   the gang's hideout.
8 The boss's manner turned decidedly ....
   after I told her I was looking for a new job.
9 I got home to find everyone in .... of tears
   over the terrible news.
10 'Is Nick pleased about his new job?'
   'Pleased? He's on .... nine!'

2 Contrast links

▶**Study Box, SB page 27**

Complete the sentences using the linking words in the
box below. The first one has been done as an example.

while/whereas	although	in contrast
on the other hand	~~but~~	yet

1 Mick likes playing tennis, *but* only if he wins!
2 Dogs are loving and loyal, ... cats are very
   independent.
3 Hugo claims to be a strict vegetarian and
   .... he regularly eats chicken!
4 Cars produce a great deal of pollution. Bicycles,
   ...., are totally environmentally friendly.
5 Checkers is a relatively easy game to master,
   .... learning to play chess takes a very long
   time.
6 Ms Ross will be able to see you tomorrow
   .... not before 11am.
7 Some people regard television as no more than
   'chewing gum for the eyes', ... many others
   appreciate its educative value.
8 .... Jo likes living in the country, she does
   miss the convenience of living in town.

3 Collocations

Complete the following sentences to form common
word combinations. The first letter of the missing word
is given in each case to help you. See the example.

1 Unfortunately, I missed the bus so I had to hitch a *lift*.
2 The lorry drivers' strike brought the traffic to a
   s................... in most parts of the country.
3 Quick! Grab h................... of my hand and I'll try
   and pull you out.
4 I took a................... of the sales to buy myself a
   smart new suit.
5 Jan takes large doses of Vitamin C at the slightest
   h................... of a cold.
6 My kids just never g................... a second thought
   to where all the money comes from to pay for their
   toys and presents.
7 Clean, running water plays a vital r................... in
   the health of the population of any country.

4 Prepositions

Complete these sentences with a preposition and the appropriate form of a word taken from the box below. See the example.

increase	tears	admission	warn	clear
stand-by	action	~~count~~		illusions	fit

1 Dan's rather mean. He thinks a box of chocolates *counts as* a generous wedding present!
2 In rough weather the coast guard is .... constant .... to respond quickly to distress signals from boats.
3 A local woman .... us .... swimming in the bay. She said sharks had been seen there recently.
4 Most people regarded his refusal to answer the question as an .... his guilt.
5 The workers were rather cynical after the meeting. Most of them were .... no .... that the management would take their complaints seriously.
6 Before applying the solution, make sure the surface to be treated has been .... all loose rust and paint.
7 The police moved swiftly .... to stop fighting between the rival groups of football fans.
8 There has been a dramatic .... the number of cases of skin cancer due to the damage to the ozone layer.
9 It was such a sad film that we were all reduced .... at the end.
10 The new model is .... electric windows, a sun-roof and a catalytic converter as standard.

5 Writing – Formal letter

Fred Smith is writing a letter to Mr Clough, the Chairman of the town council in Loxley. The information in his letter is correct but the style is far too informal. Rewrite the letter in a more formal style and include the phrases in the box below.

> I am writing to express my concern about …
> I must insist that you …
> I must urge you to …

10 North Parade
Loxley

Dear Mr Clough

I'm writing to say just how fed up I am with the state of the road outside my house. It's a real mess! Just the other day old Mrs Bicknell, the woman who lives next door, got the back wheel of her Mini stuck in one of the huge great pot-holes outside my gate. The poor old thing was really upset and we had to get two chaps from the garage to pull her car out!

Now why have we got these pot-holes in the road? Well, because of that terrible weather we had with all that ice and snow. But that was two months ago now, and I know you know about the situation because we saw a chap from the council inspecting the road just after the weather got better.

So, why haven't you done anything about it? I think you'd better send a road repair team round here as soon as possible. Not only that, I think it would be a good idea for you to be better prepared in the future so you can get things sorted out a bit more quickly!

Hoping to hear from you very soon about this problem.

Fred Smith

6 Spelling – That can't be right!

In the following sentences some of the <u>underlined</u> verbs are spelt incorrectly. Correct any mistakes, as in the example.

1 I've got a terrible memory, I keep <u>forgeting</u> that *forgetting* girl's name.

2 If you believe what they say in the commercials, some of these face creams seem to stop the <u>ageing</u> process completely!

3 William is <u>studing</u> modern languages. He hopes to become an interpreter.

4 I think the best sport for all-round fitness must be <u>swiming</u>.

5 I wish you'd stop <u>biting</u> your nails – it's a really unpleasant habit!

6 Come on, let's go to the pub, I'm <u>dieing</u> for a drink!

7 I see the police have arrested those men who are supposed to have <u>kidnaped</u> that little boy.

8 The crash is a complete mystery. It <u>occurred</u> on a sunny afternoon, with excellent visibility and practically no wind.

9 Louise must have left her credit card behind when she <u>payed</u> for the petrol.

10 They <u>tryed</u> not to laugh at his accent but just couldn't help it.

11 Jim and Fay don't seem to be getting on very well these days, they're always <u>argueing</u> about something.

12 Excuse me, Professor. Could you repeat the name of that German scientist you <u>refered</u> to earlier?

13 When I was a boy, I <u>plaied</u> rugby not football.

14 Oh Brian! You really must stop <u>disagreeing</u> with everything I say!

15 Although the fire was very small, everyone <u>paniced</u> and rushed out of the cinema, causing complete chaos.

STUDY TIP Doubling consonants

▶ Remember that in verbs of more than one syllable the final consonant is (usually) doubled only if the stress is on the syllable before it:

	○ ●		● ○
e.g.	referred	but	offered
	● ○		○ ● ○
	forgetting	but	remembering

7 Grammar

7.1 Review of passives and causative (*have/ get something done*) ▶ Focus on Grammar SB, page 30

STUDY TIP Causative *have/get*

▶ *Have/get something done* (Causative) is used to mean:
● cause something to be done by someone else
e.g. I had/got my hair cut yesterday. (The hairdresser did it.)
● cause something to happen yourself
e.g. I'll have/get this mess cleared up in no time.
● experience something (usually undesirable)
e.g. Clara had/got her credit cards stolen the other day.
Get is used rather than *have*:
● to show a feeling of obligation or urgency
e.g. I must get my car insurance renewed – it ran out last week!
● to show that something was difficult to do/achieve
e.g. We finally got the decorating finished just before we moved in.
● to indicate a planned action to achieve something
e.g. He got himself elected President of the club.
● in imperatives
e.g. Get this room cleaned up at once!

In the following sentences, decide which of the <u>underlined</u> forms is correct/more probable or if both are possible. See the example given.

1 Our house is <u>being</u>/<u>getting</u> renovated so we're staying with friends at the moment.

2 Frank's nose <u>was</u>/<u>got</u> broken while he was playing rugby.

3 The new museum on Bath Road <u>was</u>/<u>got</u> designed by Isobel Fischer.

13

4 Sorry I'm late but I kept <u>being/getting</u> lost on the way here.

5 I'm afraid the meeting will have to <u>be/get</u> postponed until next week.

6 Apart from the terrible hotel and the dirty beach, my camcorder <u>was/got</u> stolen on the last day too!

7 <u>Have/Get</u> your hair cut, you horrible little man!

8 I went to five different shops but I just couldn't <u>have/get</u> my watch repaired.

9 We eventually managed to <u>have/get</u> the tent put up just before it started snowing.

10 Don't worry, we'll soon <u>have/get</u> your car started.

7.2 Passives for formal effect

Using the verbs in the box below, complete the sentences to make more formal equivalents of the sentences provided. An example is given.

address to	~~pay for~~	accompany	receive	notify
pay	grant	accompany	require	allow

1 If you break anything, you'll have to pay for it.
All breakages *(will) have to be paid for.*

2 You might have to show some sort of ID.
Proof of identity may ....
....

3 You can't pay by cheque unless you've got a guarantee card.
All cheques must ....
....

4 You mustn't use a flash inside the cathedral.
Flash photography ....
....

5 You should tell the manager if you've got anything to complain about.
All complaints ....
....

6 They'll tell you before the end of the month if you've got the job or not.
The successful applicant ....
....

7 You've got to pay for everything within ten working days.
Full payment ....
....

8 Sorry, but the council has turned down your planning permission.
We regret to inform you that planning permission
....
....

9 You won't get any compensation if you post money and it gets lost.
No compensation ....
....

10 They don't let kids in without a grown-up.
Children ....
....

8 Dependent prepositions

Complete the following sentences with the correct preposition. See the example given.

1 All new models have been fitted *with* a safety lock.

2 You look really scruffy. Can't you tuck your shirt .... your trousers at least?

3 The main part of the house is very old. It dates .... more than 400 years.

4 The sudden movement of the train threw me .... balance and I fell head-first down the steps.

5 Erica is an excellent colleague. She goes .... her job calmly and efficiently.

6 The school ran .... financial trouble when 80% of the staff went on strike.

7 As soon as the President stepped out of the car, guards moved .... action to hold back the crowds.

8 The price of shares in the company went up .... over 50% when they announced the discovery of the new oilfield.

9 We've decided to switch .... electricity .... solar power in an attempt to be more eco-friendly.

10 The over-use of fertilisers and pesticides is one of the greatest threats .... wildlife today.

9 Wordcheck – Weather

Complete the crossword. One has been done for you.

Across

1 If severe weather or a transport problem prevents you from leaving a place, you are .... (8)
2 Violent form of 8 across with strong circular 9 across. (7)
3 Very strong 9 across. (4)
4 A great amount of water in a place that is usually dry. (5)
5 A pile of snow blown up by 9 across. (5)
6 Medical term for when your body temperature falls to a dangerously low level. (11)
7 Water at 0°C. (3)
8 Bad weather with a lot of rain. (5)
9 A current of air moving across the earth's surface. (4)
10 Blocked in by heavy snow. (9)

Down

11 Having become hard or stiff from cold. (6)
12 Periods of dry weather causing suffering and hardship. (8)
13 A violent hurricane that occurs in the western Pacific. (7)
14 A large mass of snow that slides down the side of a mountain. (9)
15 To die under water because you can't breathe. (5)
16 Heavy snowfall with extremely strong 9 across. (8)
17 A mixture of rain and snow. (5)

3 ▶ Time Eaters

1 Vocabulary – Register and style

Language Focus, SB page 36

1.1 Good monolingual dictionaries always indicate if a word or phrase has a particular 'register', in other words the type of context it should be used in. Different dictionaries use slightly different labels to indicate register but they all tell you whether the word or phrase is informal, formal, specialised/technical (e.g. medical, legal, literary, etc), old-fashioned/dated, slang, etc. Words and phrases with no label are of neutral register.

Use your monolingual dictionary to determine the register of the following words and to discover a more common/neutral (near) synonym. An example is given.

	Word	Register	Synonym
1	lesion	*medical*	*cut, wound*
2	podgy	....	....
3	bananas (adj)	....	....
4	pen (v)	....	....
5	wireless (n)	....	....
6	larceny	....	....
7	pretty (adv)	....	....
8	court (v)	....	....
9	notwithstanding	....	....
10	nosh-up	....	....
11	politic	....	....
12	bamboozle	....	....
13	clavicle	....	....
14	lingo	....	....

1.2 Make any necessary changes to the <u>underlined</u> words in the sentences that follow. Not all the underlined words are in inappropriate register. The first one has been done for you.

1 Unfortunately, he ended his days in an institution for the criminally ~~bananas~~. *insane*
2 Oh no! I think I've put my <u>clavicle</u> out again.
3 <u>Lingo</u> study classes are from 0900 to 1215 with options in the afternoon.
4 You are invited to a <u>nosh-up</u> to celebrate the 25th anniversary of the foundation of the club.
5 It's no good trying to <u>bamboozle</u> me. I'm not going to buy any insurance.

6 She turned out to be a great boss to work for <u>notwithstanding</u> what everybody said about her.
7 It is, to say the very least, <u>pretty</u> regrettable that the Managing Director has decided to resign at this crucial time.
8 <u>Podgy</u> children run a higher risk of heart disease in later life.
9 My grandmother never bought a TV. She was quite happy listening to her <u>wireless</u>, as she used to call it.
10 Can you <u>pen</u> a quick shopping list for me? You know how forgetful I am.
11 One feels it may not be <u>politic</u> at this moment to press for an increase in salary.
12 'Hi, Karen. So this is your new boyfriend.'
    'Yeah, we've been <u>courting</u> for about two months now.'
13 I'm a bit worried about Harry, doctor. He's got some nasty <u>lesions</u> on his legs.
14 'I see Fred Gomm's been arrested again.'
    'Oh, what for this time?'
    'The usual – <u>larceny</u>.'

2 *no matter …*

▶ Study Box, SB page 42

Match the first part of each sentence in Column A with the second part in Column B and add a suitable word to complete it. Look at the example.

A   *F*

1 No matter *how* hard I try, ☐
2 Well, it looks as though we'll have to buy a new one, ☐
3 She never gets to work on time, ☐
4 Don't trust her an inch, ☐
5 No matter .... much he'd like to, ☐
6 No matter .... you get there, ☐
7 No matter .... the doctor tells him, ☐
8 Cigarettes are extremely bad for you, ☐
9 Look, this rumour is totally untrue, ☐
10 Come on, you'd better clear up this mess, ☐

B

A no matter .... she promises.
B no matter .... it costs.
C he'll never forget the crash.
D no matter .... fault it was.
E he refuses to give up eating fatty food.

F   I never lose any weight.

G   no matter .... told you.

H   no matter .... bus she takes.

I   give us a ring to let us know everything's OK.

J   no matter .... little tar they might contain.

3 Grammar

3.1 *will* vs *going to* ▶ Focus on Grammar, SB page 44

Complete the sentences below using the most appropriate form of *will* or *going to* and the verb given in brackets. The first one has been done as an example.

1   What *are you going to do* (do) after you leave university?

2   I hope I .... (have) a better job this time next year.

3   Look out, that lorry's coming straight at us! Oh no, we .... (crash)!

4   'Could I have an orange juice?'
    'I'm sorry, we've run out.'
    'Oh, alright I .... (have) a coke then, please.'

5   What time do you think you .... (get) back from the conference?

6   Oh come on, look at that beautiful blue sky – it .... (not rain) today!

7   'Have you got any plans for Friday night?'
    'Not really, I .... (just stay) in and read a book.'

8   Sid promised to come and help us but he .... (probably not remember), you know how unreliable he is.

9   'Maria, the phone's ringing and I'm in the bath.'
    'OK, I .... (get) it!'

10 Quick! Give me a paper tissue, I .... (sneeze) again!

3.2 Future time clauses ▶ Focus on Grammar, SB page 44

Complete the following passage by putting the time conjunctions from the box in the correct space. The first one is shown as an example.

until	when	by the time	~~before~~	if
after	while	as soon as	until	once

Memorandum

from **Security Supervisor I B Shadow**

(1) *Before* the Ambassador arrives, you will have searched the embassy and grounds for anything suspicious. (2) .... he steps out of his bullet-proof limousine, you and three of your men will be in charge of his personal safety (3) .... he gets back into his limousine after the meeting. (4) .... he's shaken hands with the British diplomats, one of you will have to stay very close to him (5) .... he greets the well-wishers in the crowd and, remember, (6) .... you see anyone behaving strangely, you'll be expected to act first and ask questions later. (7) .... he goes inside the embassy building with the negotiators, you'll accompany him to the meeting room door and wait outside (8) .... he re-emerges – this could take anything from two to three hours. (9) .... he comes out of the embassy, the crowd will probably have dwindled somewhat but this is the time when you and your men will need to be most vigilant, so keep him covered all the time. (10) .... he gets back in his limousine, he'll be back in the hands of the mobile security unit and you'll be able to breathe a sigh of relief.

3.3 Guess the ending ▶ Focus on Grammar, SB page 44

Complete these sentences in a logical way. Look at the example provided.

1 Don't worry, you'll recognise me as soon as *you see me!*
2 It's OK, I'll wait for you until ....
3 I'll go and have a cup of tea while ....
4 Hurry up, or they'll have finished dinner by the time .... !
5 I'll meet you back here after we ....
6 Won't you get a fine if .... ?
7 Come on, let's do the washing-up before we ....
8 You won't feel much on this side of your mouth until the injection ....

3.4 Present tenses

Put the verbs in brackets into either the present simple or the present continuous tense. Put any other words in the brackets in the correct place. The first one has been done for you.

1 This milk *doesn't smell* (not smell) too fresh – I think I'll throw it out.
2 You .... (forever/use) my razor, can't you buy one of your own?
3 Oh yes, Jean and I .... (know) each other very well.
4 Mark .... (go) to work by train while his car's at the mechanic's.
5 Don't forget the coach .... (leave) at 6.45 tomorrow morning so you'd better get an early night.

6 'Where's Harry?' 'In the study, I think he .... (write) some letters.'
7 Aunt Agnes is very generous, she .... (always/give) the children wonderful presents for their birthdays.
8 That new postman .... (not seem) very bright to me, he .... (always/leave) our letters in the wrong letterbox.
9 I'm sorry we can't make it to the party on Saturday but we .... (have) dinner with some old friends.
10 Predictably, at the end of the film the Swarzenegger hero .... (rescue) the prisoners and .... (get) the girl!
11 Where .... you .... (live) until your new house is ready?
12 Carter .... (serve), Pampas .... (return) but the ball .... (go) into the net. Game to Carter.

3.5 Modal verbs ▶Focus on Grammar, SB page 48

Complete the following sentences with a suitable form of *can, could, be able, may, might, must* and the verb in brackets. An example is given.

1 I feel absolutely awful. I think I *must have* (have) flu.

2 Are you going to .... (come) to Charlie's birthday party next Saturday?

3 My word! It .... (take) you ages to write all this. There are more than 2,000 pages!

4 Which bus do you think you .... (leave) your bag on?

5 'It's odd we haven't received that cheque. Showerings said they'd sent it.'
'Yes, I suppose it .... (get) lost in the post but I doubt it.'

6 I .... (swim) really well when I was six years old.

7 Although she had a broken leg, she .... (swim) to the shore.

8 You .... (tell) me it was a formal party. I looked a real idiot in my pullover and jeans!

9 It's not surprising we .... (not find) the house. You gave us the wrong address!

10 I used to .... (run) for miles. Now I .... (not even run) round the block!

11 'I wonder why Pam ignored me in the street this morning.'
'Well, she .... (not realise) it was you. She's as blind as a bat.'

12 Smoking .... (cause) all sorts of physical problems.

13 We .... (not be) more delighted when we heard the news. Congratulations!

14 Quick, Phil! .... you (see) that man over there? I think he .... well (be) the one the police are looking for.

15 Marsha .... (be) a brilliant lawyer but she gave it all up to go and live in Nepal.

16 'What's that there in those trees?'
'It .... (not be) a dog, it's too big. Let's run for it!'

17 Jane's not completely deaf but she .... (not hear) properly for a long time.

18 Billy, come away from that dog. It .... (bite) you.

STUDY TIP *could* vs *was able to*

▶ Remember *could* is used to show general ability in the past:
e.g. She could drive when she was 13.
▶ *was able to* shows ability on a specific occasion in the past:
e.g. Despite having a flat tyre, she was able to drive home.

4 ▶ Stress

1 Cause and effect

▶**Study Box, SB page 55**

Match the beginning of each sentence in Column A with the correct ending in Column B and add any necessary words. See the example.

A

1 Careless driving   *I*
2 Eating too many sugary things
3 Skin cancer
4 Heart attacks
5 One .... of using a computer all day
6 Bad posture
7 A sudden rise in temperature
8 Malaria can .... from
9 Obesity can be the .... of
10 Crimes in inner cities have increased
11 Letting children always do what they want
12 Accidents in the home

B

A overeating and a lack of exercise.
B can be .... to tiredness and distraction.
C can and does .... in tooth decay.
D is to cause headaches and eye problems.
E being bitten by a mosquito.
F is a major .... of chronic back pain.
G .... of high unemployment and a lack of recreational facilities.
H can be .... by sunbathing for long periods.
I is a major *cause* of road accidents.
J can and does .... to behavioural problems at school.
K have increased as a .... of our modern stressful lifestyles.
L can and does .... avalanches.

2 Grammar

▶**Focus on Grammar, SB page 58**

2.1 *-ing* forms

In each of the following sentences add a suitable subject made from a verb. The first one is shown as an example.

1 *Drinking lots of water* is supposed to be good for your complexion.
2 .... causes a lot of unnecessary accidents every year.
3 .... is much less popular now than it was 20 years ago.
4 .... is by far the most common way of spending the evening.
5 .... often makes you appreciate the things you took for granted in your own country.
6 .... crossword puzzles is a classic time-eater.
7 .... is a good way of losing weight and getting fit.
8 .... in poor light can damage your eyesight.
9 .... is my favourite way of relaxing.
10 .... is a sign of nervousness or stress.

2.2 Prepositions and conjunctions + -ing

Complete the following sentences by adding the correct preposition and a suitable gerund. See the example.

1 I'm really looking forward *to meeting* your sister, I've heard so much about her.
2 We're thinking .... to Turkey this summer.
3 Arnold was falsely accused .... cash from the till.
4 When I was a child my mother was always warning me .... lifts from strangers.
5 Jean doesn't believe .... today what she can put off until tomorrow!
6 Trevor is absolutely hopeless .... photos – he always cuts your head or feet off!
7 Lesley's rather anxious .... the doctor next week – she thinks it might be something serious.
8 Emma was furious with me .... her ex-boyfriend to the party.
9 I intend to find out who's responsible .... the window.
10 I'm tired .... the same old faces every day – I need a change!
11 Anyone interested .... on the trip to Bath should tell Kerry by noon today.
12 Dr Farquar is famous .... people's names – I'm surprised he can remember his own!
13 Carol is incredibly honest. She'd never dream .... a lie.
14 You can delete anything you don't want .... this button.
15 Sally found it difficult to re-adjust to the British way of life .... back from a long holiday in the Greek islands.
16 What's the name of that stuff you use .... grass stains out of clothes?
17 MANUFACTURER'S WARNING: Always wear safety goggles .... this machinery.
18 Francesco picked up a strong American accent .... a Master's degree in the USA.
19 .... practically nothing, I just can't seem to lose any weight!
20 You must check in your mirror .... another car on the motorway.

2.3 -ing or infinitive?

Complete the following sentences with either a gerund or infinitive. In some cases the verb to use is indicated in brackets. The first one has been done for you.

1 You'll remember *to fill* the car up with petrol, won't you?
2 Try .... a cup of camomile tea before you go to bed.
3 She remembered .... his face in a police identikit picture.
4 You must try .... down on the number of cigarettes you smoke.
5 Being a doctor means .... very long hours and .... a fragmented social life.
6 During the meeting we came .... that not only were we not getting a pay rise but probably a pay cut!
7 I regret .... him he was pathetic, I got a bit angry, that's all.
8 I regret .... you that there is very little chance of recovery.
9 Having defeated the champion in the opening match, she went on .... the tournament.
10 Isn't it time you stopped .... on your parents so much and tried .... on your own two feet?
11 You can't expect .... the exam if you spend all day .... video games.
12 I can't help .... (wonder) why Julie keeps .... home so late.
13 It's no good .... (worry) about things you can't be expected .... (know).
14 Would you mind not .... in here? I can't stand .... in other people's cigarette smoke.
15 I hate .... in small, confined places. I was once trapped in a lift and tried .... (smash) the doors down.
16 Don't forget .... the car to the garage on Monday – the brakes need .... again.
17 It's not worth .... (risk) .... (get) a fine by .... the car here even for five minutes.
18 There was no point in .... (promise) .... (help) if you don't like .... (get) your hands dirty!

2.4 *-ing* nouns

Put the correct form of the nouns in the box below in the correct places in the following sentences. See the example given.

showing	sighting	saying	setting	awakening
spelling	carving	~~hanging~~	following	fitting
airing	being	hearing	recording	reading

1 A hundred years ago people used to attend public *hangings* outside local jails.
2 We'll need to leave work early if we want to see the earlier .... of the new movie.
3 The rock group 'U2' has a very large .... all over the world.
4 Have there ever been any verified .... of the Loch Ness monster?
5 I like to throw open the windows and give the room a good .... every morning.
6 Our second .... this evening comes from the poetic works of Oscar Wilde.
7 There's a lot of truth in the .... 'Everything comes to he who waits'.
8 We bought a beautiful wooden .... of a horse in Hungary.
9 The cabins were in the most attractive ...., on the edge of a lake, surrounded by forest.
10 He felt a gradual .... of love for this strange, independent girl.
11 There was an official .... to discover who was responsible for polluting the river.
12 Actually, the word has two different .... and both are correct!
13 He told me he'd spoken to some alien .... from another universe!
14 The bathroom still has all the original Victorian ....
15 I'm sorry it's so crackly but it's the original 1948 concert ....

2.5 *-ing* adjectives

Match each adjective in Column A with the appropriate noun in Column B. The first one is shown as an example.

	A			**B**
1	carving	G	A	board
2	shaving	☐	B	rod
3	building	☐	C	bag
4	diving	☐	D	stone
5	watering	☐	E	licence
6	parking	☐	F	powder
7	driving	☐	G	knife
8	filling	☐	H	can
9	paving	☐	I	water
10	walking	☐	J	site
11	fishing	☐	K	cream
12	sleeping	☐	L	space
13	ironing	☐	M	station
14	washing	☐	N	stick
15	drinking	☐	O	board

STUDY TIP Collocations

▶ Some common words are very useful in forming collocations e.g. *board, card, bag.*

diving	chess	chopping	BOARD
birthday	credit	membership	CARD
carrier	shoulder	shopping	BAG

▶ Keep a record of these and other such useful words and their possible partners.

---

3 Word building – Verb formation

Use the nouns or adjectives shown in brackets to form suitable verbs to fill each space. An example is provided.

1 If you tell the company exactly what you want, they can put together a *customised* (custom) computer system for you.
2 Would it be possible to .... (large) this part of the photo?
3 You'll never get a job unless you .... (smart) yourself up a bit.
4 It was really Charles Dickens who .... (popular) the celebration of Christmas in Britain.
5 If you're worried about the drinking water, there are

tablets you can get to .... (pure) it.

6 We don't need to hear all the details of the meeting. Could you just .... (summary) the main point for us?

7 Everyone now agrees that smoking .... (danger) people's health.

8 Frank bought an old car and .... (cannibal) it to repair two others.

9 We were all .... (horror) by the amount of money we had to pay.

10 The management are trying to persuade the workers to agree to .... (long) the working week.

11 Excuse me, professor. Could you .... (clear) what you mean by 'dumbing down'?

12 Taking regular exercise can .... (less) the risk of heart disease.

13 The police find it extremely difficult to .... (force) speed limits out of town.

14 Gangs of hooligans have been .... (terror) local residents.

15 Our anger .... (height) still further as we realised our luggage had been taken to the wrong airport.

4 Dependent prepositions

Replace the incorrect prepositions in the following sentences with the correct ones. The first one is shown as an example.

1 You can reduce your vulnerability ~~for~~ *to* stress by taking a nap in the afternoon.

2 I play tennis – but just in fun. I'm not very good at it.

3 I've no idea why Tony is so angry. He never confides with me.

4 Jane's out in the garden mulling through a problem to do with work.

5 There's no need to exercise at the point of exhaustion.

6 At weekends, I like to immerse myself with the peace and quiet of the countryside.

7 Bob's finding it hard to focus his mind in his studies at the moment.

8 Dentists fall on the category of high-stress occupations.

9 One of the greatest causes of stress at the workplace is the feeling of being undervalued.

10 Moving house often has a negative effect for people's mental health.

5 Collocations

Complete each of the following sentences with the correct form of an appropriate verb taken from the box. The first one is shown as an example.

modify	receive	meet	provide
calm	do	organise	answer
take	~~spend~~	attend	

1 We all need to *spend* some time just enjoying ourselves.

2 Not having enough money to .... your basic needs is a great cause of stress.

3 Many people find it hard to .... their behaviour in order to reduce stress.

4 We've just been told that the new multi-gym will .... facilities for just about all indoor sports.

5 Excuse me! I wonder if you'd have the time to .... a brief questionnaire.

6 I try to .... my mind by .... yoga.

7 How many alcoholic drinks do you .... per week?

8 It's important to both give and .... affection regularly.

9 I really must try and .... my time better. I'm always leaving things until the last minute.

10 Her grandmother is in excellent health and regularly .... the local sports club.

6 Wordcheck – Stress and relaxation

6.1 Odd word out

<u>Underline</u> the word in each group that does not fit in with the other three. Use a dictionary to help you if necessary. The first one is shown as an example.

1 fun	enjoyable	<u>friendly</u>	light-hearted
2 nap	rush	snooze	siesta
3 dizzy	worn out	tired	run-down
4 tackle	wrestle with	fight	mull over
5 focus	unwind	relax	switch off
6 source	result	cause	reason
7 tense	angry	upset	vulnerable
8 stuck	confined	boosted	cramped

6.2 Collocations

Match up the word partners in Columns A and B as in the example.

A		B	
1 blood	C	A	nights
2 stomach		B	effects
3 time		C	pressure
4 stress		D	breakdown
5 minor		E	ulcers
6 balanced		F	constraints
7 sleepless		G	trouble
8 nervous		H	ailments
9 heart		I	meal
10 harmful		J	overload

▶ Progress Test One

Units 1–4

1 Structural cloze

Complete the following newspaper article by writing one word in each of the numbered gaps.

Shining example or white elephant?

The new university hospital in Trenton, (1) .... the Health Minister Victoria Culley has described (2) .... a 'shining example' to hospitals all (3) .... the country, has been open now for over six months. (4) .... heard several less than complimentary comments about the organisation and efficiency of the place, I decided to see for myself. Before (5) .... there, I had arranged with my local GP to have some routine blood tests for anaemia.

In (6) .... of arriving early (7.15 a.m.!) I found that there were already long queues at the reception desks. (7) .... I was waiting, I looked around and have to admit that it is an impressive building; large and light with marble everywhere. Eventually my turn came and I presented my doctor's letters to the receptionist, (8) .... informed me that I was in the X-ray queue and I'd have to go to another queue and start again! I couldn't believe it and asked her if it (9) .... be possible to give me an appointment card anyway (10) .... making me queue up again. She informed me it was no (11) .... arguing with her and I should have read the sign, an almost invisible piece of card saying 'X-rays'

just in front of her (12) .... very few people can have seen it. No (13) .... how hard I tried to persuade her, she wouldn't give me an appointment card for a blood test, so I started (14) .... again and finally got the card at 8.30! I then set off for the blood tests room, following the nice new signs (15) .... they suddenly stopped and I realised that I was in a part of the hospital that hasn't been finished yet! When I got to the door I saw a notice saying 'Back in 10 minutes'. I sat down and waited for 30 minutes before a doctor appeared and told me to come in without, of course, (16) .... for keeping me waiting. I asked him why I'd had to wait and he explained he'd had to help out in another ward which was (17) .... as a (18) .... of a flu epidemic among the doctors!

I got out of the hospital at 9.45 a.m. and breathed a sigh of relief. I'm now waiting for the results.

So, Mrs Culley, a far from rosy picture. Certainly the public should be (19) .... no illusions that things have changed for the better. Perhaps you should visit the hospital as an anonymous out-patient rather than a government minister if you really want to know what it's like, (20) .... , as I suspect, you don't actually care that much!

---

2 Phrasal verbs

Complete each of the following sentences with the appropriate form of a suitable phrasal verb. An example is provided.

Example: Dennis has given up his job so he can stay at home and *look after* the children.

1 Overeating and lack of exercise can .... serious health problems in later life.
2 Hi Brenda, Peter here. I'm just .... to say I've got two tickets for the concert on Saturday night. Fancy coming?
3 You should .... the pros and cons carefully before buying a second-hand car.
4 Now, don't .... us .... We're counting on you to cook something really special for the party this Saturday.
5 The group .... the concert with their greatest hits. So everyone went home happy.

3 Error correction

In most of the lines of the following text, there is one unnecessary word. It is either grammatically incorrect or does not fit in with the sense of the text. For each numbered line 1–16, find this word and write it in the space to the right of the text. Some lines are correct. Indicate these lines with a tick (✓) in the space. The exercise begins with two examples (0).

Hibernation syndrome

I don't know about you, but come to the winter months, my body
seems to require more sleep than in summer and I'm definitely at
my happiest when I'm being curled up in a hedgehog-style ball.
'Wanting to sleep more in winter is not natural and nothing to
worry about, unless you are sleeping for more than 12 hours a
day,' says sleep expert Dr James B. Maas. The reason for we feel
drowsy has as much to do with our biochemistry as it does so with
wanting to sniggle up like a couch potato indoors. 'It's all to do
with melatonin,' explains Dr Maas, 'a hormone with which is
secreted by the brain's pineal gland in response to darkness.'
They may feel more sleepy, but as many people find getting to
sleep in winter is a problem. It's hardly surprising. When lounging
around indoors drinking mugs of warming up coffee and snacking
on chocolate bars doesn't always prepare you for a good
night's rest. If you do have trouble nodding off, Deepak Chopra
has this tip. 'Try a soothing mix of the sweet and sour
essential oils, such as orange, geranium and clove are mixed with
almond oil and rubbed it on to your forehead just before bedtime.'

0	*to*
0	✓
1	....
2	....
3	....
4	....
5	....
6	....
7	....
8	....
9	....
10	....
11	....
12	....
13	....
14	....
15	....
16	....

4 Word formation

Read the texts below. Use the words in the box to form one word that fits in the numbered space in the texts. The exercise begins with an example.

All at sea

Just after sunrise, Jack looked out of the porthole again. If anything, the sea was looking even (0) *choppier* than it had been the night before. The wind had (1) .... and was now accompanied by (2) .... rain. Jack's heart sank. He felt (3) .... after yet another (4) .... night spent tying things down and praying the yacht wouldn't sink under the relentless battering of the wind and the waves. With the radio broken, he had no chance of signalling for help and all he had for company was mile upon (5) .... mile of mountainous seas between him and the (6) .... of port. He realised he was in a (7) .... situation.

0	CHOPPY
1	INTENSE
2	TORRENT
3	DREAD
4	SLEEP
5	END
6	SAFE
7	DESPAIR

Homeopathy

Our army of (8) .... and underpaid family doctors are daily disheartened to see the same people returning with the same problems. They know only too well that thousands of people suffer from (9) .... for which conventional treatment proves (10) .... , no matter how many expensive or painful tests they are forced to (11) .... However, all is not lost. Alternative medicine and, (12) .... , homeopathy is gaining (13) .... as a valid form of treatment even though it remains hard to prove (14) .... just how it works! Sceptics regard it as a fairly (15) .... form of hocus-pocus with active ingredients so diluted they wouldn't hurt a fly. But with so many devotees, it seems hard to ignore its potential any longer.

8	WORK
9	AIL
10	EFFECT
11	GO
12	PARTICULAR
13	RECOGNISE
14	SCIENCE
15	HARM

5 Discourse cloze

For questions 1–6, read through the following text and then choose from the list A–J the best phrase or sentence to fill each of the spaces. Write one letter (A–J) in the correct space. Some of the answers do not fit at all. The exercise begins with an example (0).

So how was your inbox this morning? Overflowing at the seams? Full of messages from people you don't know, subjects you don't care about, and (0) ..I. , the odd gem of information which could transform your life (1) .... ?

Welcome to the club: e-mail is both business blessing and commercial curse. You can't do without it, yet you still can't face the idea of wading through every one of those tedious messages that come through the digital door every day. Perhaps (2) .... , then it's time to move on to the fun parts of the magazine because I have momentous news for you: the e-mail flood may be bad today, but tomorrow (3) .... . Not only are you going to get more of the stuff, the stuff itself is going to explode too – into audio and graphics, video and customer response forms. And (4) .... , you're going to lose a key business edge along the way.

In the US, (5) .... for large corporations that deal with employees, customers and suppliers by e-mail to dispatch a staggering 800,000 messages per day (yes, you did read that correctly). Small wonder that one boss of a large software company decided to close down his network e-mail system for part of each day, (6) .... he thought people were too busy e-mailing and not spending enough time communicating.

A if all this sounds way too familiar
B it is not unknown
C unless you refuse to use it
D precisely because
E if you try to ignore it
F it's going to be ten times worse
G despite the fact that
H if only you could find it
 I somewhere in among the dross

5 ▶ Globe Trotting

1 Cohesive devices

▶ **Language Focus, SB page 65**

Correct any illogical linking devices in the following sentences. The first one is shown as an example.

Although
1 ~~Because~~ he'd never tried it before he was very good at it.
2 Don't forget to phone us finally you get there.
3 Despite being an accomplished musician, Freda is also a first-rate painter.
4 As well as the bad weather, the race meeting has been cancelled.
5 I hope to get some work done while the holidays.
6 So that you're always borrowing a pen, I've decided to buy you one.
7 Cars are expensive to maintain, whereas bicycles cost very little.
8 I put the vases on top of the piano since they wouldn't get broken.
9 While a little sunshine can be good for you, too much can be very harmful.
10 The job is a little tedious, but however it offers lots of fringe benefits.
11 Credit may be arranged so as to spread payment over twelve months.
12 Tony has decided to take a year off owing to travel around the world.

2 Grammar

▶ **Focus on Grammar, SB page 70**

2.1 Past simple vs past continuous

In the following sentences put the verbs in brackets in either the past simple or past continuous tense. Put any other words in the brackets in the correct place. Look at the example provided.

1 While the teacher *was explaining* (explain) the sum on the blackboard, the children *were throwing* (throw) paper aeroplanes around the classroom.
2 Eve .... (live) in Athens when she .... (meet) the man who was to become her husband.
3 .... you .... (not work) at McIlroy's when they .... (have) that terrible fire?

4 As it .... (get) foggier it .... (become) almost impossible to steer the boat along the narrow canal.
5 I .... (hear) a strange noise just as I .... (go) to sleep.
6 When the fire alarm .... (go) off, we .... (leave) the building as quickly as possible.
7 At the place where we .... (live) before, our neighbours .... (always/have) violent arguments late at night.
8 I .... (hope) you'd come round for tea one afternoon next week.
9 Fiona .... (live) in New York when her first novel .... (publish).
10 On looking out of the window, Dick .... (see) it was another dreary day. The wind .... (blow) hard and big black clouds .... (gather) on the horizon.
11 While the others .... (lie) on the beach, poor old Gary .... (work) in the office as usual.
12 When the phone .... (ring), she .... (pick) it up and .... (put) it down again!
13 I .... (never/understand) why you .... (always/get) to school late on Monday mornings.
14 Beverly .... (work) in a fast-food restaurant for a few months before she .... (go) to college.
15 When I .... (be) a lad, we .... (always/go) to Heysham for our summer holidays. I .... (really/love) the place even though it .... (often/rain).

2.2 Past perfect simple and continuous

In the following passage fill in the spaces with an appropriate form of the past perfect simple, past perfect continuous, past simple or past continuous of the verb in brackets. The first one has been done for you.

Frogs in my car

I (1) *had been waiting* (wait) for over an hour when Barry finally (2) .... (turn up) on the tractor. He (3) .... (explain) he (4) .... (hold up) by a fallen tree on the road. I (5) .... (not find) this hard to believe as a gale force wind (6) .... (blow) for the past 5 hours accompanied by torrential rain. The reason why I (7) .... (call) Barry was that my car (8) .... (lie) on its side in a ditch. I (9) .... (drive) along very slowly in the terrible weather when suddenly a large dog (10) .... (appear) in front of me. I (11) .... (brake) to avoid hitting it and the car (12) .... (skid) out of control on the water and mud on the road and into the ditch. I (13) .... (manage) to get out through the window. The problem now was that the car (14) .... (fill up) with water and mud! Within seconds Barry, who (15) .... (wear) enormous rubber boots, (16) .... (tie) a rope to the front bumper of the car and (17) .... (pull) it out with the tractor. After a few minutes the car was the right way up and back on the road again. We (18) .... (open) the door and out (19) .... (jump) two big frogs who (20) .... (swim) in through the open window!

3 Phrasal verbs

3.1 Phrasal verbs with *up*

Substitute the underlined words in the following sentences with a phrasal verb with *up*. The first one is shown as an example.

1 The TV's rather quiet, can't you <u>increase its volume</u>/*turn it up?*
2 I'd like to <u>improve</u>/..................... my Spanish before going on holiday to Valencia.
3 Come on, <u>finish your drink</u>/..................... and we'll go for a walk along the river.
4 What's the matter, Rupert? Can't you <u>fasten</u>/..................... your seatbelt for yourself?
5 In my grandparents' day it was unusual for married couples to <u>separate</u>/..................... .
6 The police eventually managed to <u>bring together</u>/..................... all the criminals who had taken part in the bank robbery.
7 Quite honestly, Mr Mitty, I think you've <u>invented</u>/..................... the whole story.
8 Children often don't realise how cruel it is to <u>unite</u>/..................... against someone who is different from them.
9 If you don't understand a word, try and guess what it means before you <u>find its meaning</u>/..................... in a dictionary.
10 Can't we <u>go a little faster</u>/..................... a bit or we'll never get there on time?

3.2 In other words

In the following story replace the words in brackets with an appropriate phrasal verb taken from the box below. See the example.

pull up	start up	go through with
look on to	pull off	rip off
build up	stub out	pull over
~~look out for~~	jump out of	pull out
drop off to	shoot off	take aback

The hold-up

The hold-up had started going wrong. Clyde, who was supposed to be (1) *looking out for* (waiting to see) the security van from a flat which (2) .... (gave a view of) the main street, had (3) .... (gone to) sleep due to the fact that he had been drinking double brandies all morning to (4) .... (increase) his courage.

So Bugsy, Danny and Studs were completely (5) .... (amazed) when the security van (6) .... (stopped) outside the bank without a word of warning from Clyde. Bugsy (7) .... (extinguished) his cigarette. 'We've gotta (8) .... it (not leave unfinished) now – it's too late to (9) .... (abandon a difficult plan)!'
Studs (10) .... (put in motion) the getaway car and (11) .... (moved) to a spot just past the bank. Bugsy and Danny (12) .... (quickly left) the car and (13) .... (ran) towards the bank. Studs suddenly realised just how shaky he felt after the recent events and got out of the car for a breath of fresh air.

A few minutes later Bugsy and Danny came running back from the bank shouting to the still dazed Studs that they had (14) .... it .... (succeeded in a difficult plan). Studs, however, didn't seem too interested and stood glued to the spot where he had left the car.

'Good God! Is nothing sacred these days? Some crook's just (15) .... the car .... (stolen)!'

3.3 Three-word phrasal verbs ▶ Study Box, SB page 72

Complete the following sentences with three-word phrasal verbs. An example is provided in number one.

1 We still haven't sold the house because the buyers went *back on* their word and pulled out of the deal.
2 As there was no official at the gate, Diana got .... not buying an entrance ticket.
3 Unfortunately, the new restaurant didn't really live .... our expectations.
4 How much longer have we got to put .... these hooligans before the police take some action?
5 I look .... meeting you at the congress next month.
6 I gave .... waiting for the landlord to repair the roof and paid for the work to be done myself.
7 Someone broke into the shop last night and made .... some videos and a TV set.
8 We spent over an hour at the airport looking .... Vera's cousin but, somehow, we missed him!
9 Although they are from very different backgrounds, they get .... each other extremely well.
10 I'm sorry I haven't got .... fixing your window yet. I'll do it tomorrow.

STUDY TIP Phrasal verbs

▶ A good way to record and remember phrasal verbs is to group them according to particle (*up, down, in, out, on, off,* etc) rather than verb (*get, make, run,* etc):
e.g. turn .... keep
       switch ON   put   UP WITH
       keep .... catch
Remember that particles often have fixed meanings such as fastening and restriction, approach etc:
e.g. wrap up, zip up, tie up, make for, head for

4 Reference links

► **Study Box, SB page 75**

Match sentences 1–9 with A–H. Use the reference links in the box below to complete A–H. Look at the example given.

| such | which | ~~the aforementioned~~ | that |
| this | the above | the latter | another |

1 Frank and Nigel Fish had been seen in the area two or three days before the robbery took place. *D*
2 The national press falls into two main camps, the broadsheets and the tabloids.
3 Occasionally the child does not want to be re-united with the parents.
4 Not recommended for people with angina, diabetes, migraine or vertigo.
5 There has been a family feud going on for about ten years.
6 Hamford seems to be more and more polluted – the city centre is just appalling with all those buses belching out exhaust fumes,
7 One way of treating a headache is to take some pain killers, like aspirins.
8 Didn't you realise Andrew is only partially sighted?

A In .... cases it is extremely hard to find a solution.
B .... is to try relaxation techniques or, better still, massage.
C .... is why we've decided to move out to the countryside.
D Not only that but the style of the crime is typical of *the aforementioned* brothers.
E Oh, ... explains why it's Barbara who always drives the car!
F As you can imagine, ... makes birthdays and Christmas parties rather tense affairs!
G .... tend to concentrate on the more sensational or scandalous aspects of the news.
H Please consult your GP if you suffer from any of ....

5 Word stress – Air travel

Use a dictionary to help you mark the stress patterns in the underlined words below. Draw one circle for each syllable and show the stressed syllables with large circles. Be careful to identify the grammatical function in each case. See the example provided.

1 Oh no, I've left my handbag at the check-in desk.
   (O o above "check-in")
2 The hostess on the plane gave us some sweets to suck before take-off.
3 Would late passengers for flight BY577 please check in immediately.
4 Lavatories on planes are usually rather small.
5 The bus for the city centre leaves from outside the terminal building.
6 Please have your boarding card ready.
7 I'm not sure if I'll be leaving today as I've got a standby ticket.
8 Sorry for the delay, we hope to take off in 5 minutes.

STUDY TIP   Word stress

► Use bubbles not accents to show the correct stress on words you have difficulty with. Bubbles show not only the main stress but also the number of syllables which are actually pronounced.

e.g. comfortable, interesting, temperature

6 Writing – Formal letter

Look at the advertisement opposite, which **appeared in** *The Independent,* and the letter written in **response to** it. The letter contains 14 mistakes. Find and correct them as in the two examples provided.

COUNTRY COTTAGE HOLIDAYS

Give yourself a break in one of our beautifully restored country cottages with all mod cons – sleeping from 4 to 10 people. Prices from £100 per week.
**Contact: Randolf Jefferies
20 The Green,
Hinton,
Devon HN3 2CC.**

5 Redland Road
Barford BF2 8VR
21st May, 20—

Randolf Jefferies
20 The Green
Hinton
Devon HN3 2CC

Dear Mr ~~Randolf~~ *Jefferies*
I was most interested ~~by~~ *in* your advertisement on 'The Independent' and I am writing for obtain further informations about your country cottage holidays.

In particular, I would like knowing in which parts of the country your cottages are located as my friends and I are interested to stay as far away from large cities as possible. I would like to know too if it would be possible renting a cottage for six people for up to six months and whether pets are allowed as my friends and I have three well-behaved dogs we are planning to take with us.

I should, therefore, be terrible grateful if you will send me full details of your larger more isolated cottages and any brochures you may have.

Thanking you in advance for your help. I look forward to hear from you as early as possible.

Yours faithfully

Sandy Melville
SANDY MELVILLE

7 Editing for phrasal verbs

In the following passage most (but not all) of the phrasal verbs have either the wrong verb or wrong particle. If a correction is required, write it in the space provided. Look at the example (0).

Although £10 seemed a lot for a guided walking tour, I'd <u>charged</u> up like most of the others staying at the hotel. The tour was supposed to start at 9 o'clock, so we were getting a little angry and were just about to give in and go and have a cup of coffee together when the guide finally turned out at reception 30 minutes late. She said she had left home on time but had had to go back as she'd forgotten the tour maps – it came out to be her first day on the job! First of all, she sorted off which of us already had maps and which didn't. We eventually set off more than an hour behind schedule and started making to the old town. Although there were only about ten of us, I found it hard to hear her commentary as she seemed to have singled out the three or four people closest to her to talk to. As we were walking along I asked her if we could go and see a beautiful old church, but she replied rather abruptly that we had to stick in the itinerary. After that, I decided I'd better write down my £10 and rely on my own map and intelligence for a more personal tour of the city.	**0** *paid* **1** .... **2** .... **3** .... **4** .... **5** .... **6** .... **7** .... **8** .... **9** .... **10** .... **11** .... **12** .... **13** .... **14** .... **15** .... **16** ....

8 Wordcheck – Collocations

Complete the following sentences with suitable word combinations. See the example.

1 I've never done it before but I'll give it a *try*.
2 When I asked him where room C10 was, he just .... his shoulders and told me to ask someone else.
3 After the bank robbery, the thieves went into .... in an old barn for six months.
4 We advise all our clients to .... out travel insurance.
5 It's pretty quiet now but when the holiday season is under .... it's absolutely packed with people.
6 Ski instructors must .... fairly interesting lives, mustn't they?
7 I hope Bobby won't make himself the life and .... of the party tonight. It's so embarrassing!
8 The group's mission is to .... peace between nations and help different peoples understand each other better.
9 'Hold your .... boy! Speak when you're spoken to!', shouted the old man angrily.
10 As the inspection day approached, the manager .... us all under tremendous pressure to make sure everything was in order.

6 ▶ Language Matters

1 Relative clauses

▶ **Focus on Grammar, SB page 84**

1.1 Relative pronouns

Where possible, remove the relative pronouns in the following sentences and make any other necessary changes. Look at the example given.

1 Who's that man ~~that~~ Lisa's talking to?
2 I'm calling about the advert that appeared in yesterday's 'Evening Echo'.
3 Isn't that the hotel where Greg and Sally had their wedding reception?
4 The gentleman with whom you spoke last time is no longer with the company.
5 That's the couple whose house was burgled last week.
6 The bulldog that attacked that little girl has been destroyed.
7 The reason why the accident happened has never been clarified.
8 Is this the picture to which you were referring?
9 She always chooses a moment to call when everyone's out of the office.
10 That's the car that we were thinking of buying.

1.2 Different endings

Each of the sentences below can end in several different ways. Choose the possible endings from the box below and add a suitable relative pronoun where necessary. The first one is shown as an example.

1 What's the name of that town
a _which_ was featured in that TV documentary last week?
b ....?
c ....?
d ....?
2 Have you still got that book
a ....?
b ....?
c ....?
3 Wasn't it Elizabeth
a ....?
b ....?
c ....?
4 Which is the month
a ....?
b ....?
c ....?

> you wanted to have off
> author I can never remember the name of
> lived in China until she was 16
> had to be invented to make the year longer
> mayor was arrested for corruption
> was reviewed in *The Times* last week
> the restaurant sacked for being rude to customers
> ~~was featured in that TV documentary last week~~
> most people get married
> I lent you last term
> was almost completely destroyed during the war
> Richard Burton was born
> boyfriend wants to go and live in Italy

1.3 Reduced relative clauses

Decide which of the following sentences contain reduced relative clauses and which do not. Put a tick (✓) in the appropriate column as in the example.

Y N

1 The man called Max at the office and asked him to meet him later that day. □ ☑

2 The man called Max in the film was played by Patrick Swayze. □ □

3 Plums used to make me sick when I was a boy. □ □

4 The player hurt in the tackle had to be taken to hospital. □ □

5 Coffee made with this new percolator tastes better than ever! □ □

6 The shark attacked in the shallows, causing panic among the bathers. □ □

7 The player hurt his knee in the tackle but played on. □ □

8 Coffee made Brenda feel agitated so she gave up drinking it. □ □

9 The shark attacked in the shallows swam away losing a lot of blood. □ □

10 Plums used to make jam must be very ripe. □ □

1.4 Fill in the gaps

Complete the following sentences with a suitable reduced relative clause and any necessary prepositions. Each sentence must have a passive meaning. Look at the example given.

1 Children *born on* or before 1st September should have been vaccinated.

2 Any books .... to the library more than three days late will be subject to a fine.

3 Meat .... oil or butter contains much more cholesterol than meat which has been grilled.

4 Patients .... the new wonder drug showed no greater signs of recovery than those receiving traditional medicine.

5 Did you know that grapes .... to dry in the sun turn into raisins?

6 Tickets .... phone must be paid for within 24 hours.

7 The management declines all responsibility for property .... from cars .... this car park.

8 The skeleton .... the building site last month turned out to be over 2,000 years old.

9 Yes folks, it's true. Clothes .... new 'Spumo' won't lose their colour. We guarantee it!

10 Looking round a junk shop one day, Stanley came across a picture .... by Rembrandt.

11 Dogs .... Britain from another European country must spend three months in quarantine.

12 Baggage .... unattended may be destroyed.

2 *like, as* and *alike*

▶ Study Box, SB page 85

Put *like, as* or *alike* in the appropriate places in the following sentences. One is shown as an example.

1 Several of the businessmen got a little rowdy and started behaving *like* complete idiots.

2 Just .... I suspected, my letter had been delivered to the wrong office.

3 'The Watkins brothers are really ...., aren't they?'
   'Yes, just .... two peas in a pod.'

4 Nothing can go wrong providing you do exactly .... you're told.

5 The fundamental injustice of the law was that it did not treat all offenders ....

6 There's no need to talk .... that in front of the children!

7 .... they had feared, the company decided to make 200 workers redundant.

8 Cheryl must have been terrified. She came running out of the house .... a bat out of hell!

STUDY TIP   *as* vs *like*

▶ A useful distinction between these two is:
as = in the capacity of
e.g. She works as a taxi driver.
He used his briefcase as a table to rest his notes on.
like = similar to
e.g. She works like a beaver.
He's got a briefcase like yours.

---

3 Comparison

▶ Focus on Grammar, SB page 89

3.1 Comparatives and superlatives

Complete the following sentences with a suitable comparative or superlative form of the words in brackets. Look at the example given.

1 According to a computer, Spanish is (easy) *the easiest* foreign language to learn.
2 Dogs are intelligent but not (intelligent) .... chimpanzees.
3 They say it's (good) .... to have loved and lost than never to have loved at all.
4 Even (carefully) .... prepared plans can go wrong.
5 England isn't (mountainous country) .... Scotland.
6 Reykjavik is the world's (northern) .... capital city.
7 Your composition is full of mistakes because you didn't spend half (time) .... on it .... you should have!
8 Don't worry, you'll be OK with Gerry, he's (careful driver) .... you could wish to have.
9 In the Alto Adige region of Italy, German dialect is spoken much (frequently) .... Italian.
10 Sumo wrestlers must be (heavy) .... athletes in the world.

3.2 *as ... as*

Using a good monolingual dictionary, check which words in Column A go with the ones in Column B to form common comparative expressions with *as ... as (a) ...* Look at the example provided.

A		B	
1	pretty	G	A a pancake
2	weak	☐	B a bat
3	fresh	☐	C a kitten
4	thin	☐	D a bone
5	stubborn	☐	E an eel
6	slippery	☐	F a daisy
7	proud	☐	G a picture
8	strong	☐	H a mule
9	dry	☐	I an ox
10	deaf	☐	J a rake
11	flat	☐	K a peacock
12	blind	☐	L a post

3.3 Complete the sentences

Now complete the following sentences with the expressions you have made. The first one has been done for you.

1 Doesn't little Amy look nice in her new dress?
   Oh yes, she's *as pretty as a picture.*
2 Alf is ...., he can't see much without his glasses.
3 Oh no! We'll have to change the tyre, it's ....
4 If we don't get some rain soon, we'll never grow anything in the garden, it's ....
5 I had a good night's sleep last night, so I'm .... this morning.
6 I wouldn't give Colin any of my money to invest, he's ....
7 Tim's been in bed all week with flu and he's ....
8 Freda's ...., once she makes up her mind she's going to do something, nothing you can say will stop her!
9 'My word! David's lost a lot of weight.'
   'Yes. Do you think he's OK? He looks .... to me!'
10 'Mrs Copley's daughter has been offered a place at university.'
   'Yes and she's .... She's already told half the town.'
11 Young Alan is really helpful on the farm. He's .... and he'll do anything you ask him to.
12 I'm afraid Grandad won't hear you unless you shout. He's ....!

4 Degrees of comparison

Using the language in the boxes below, complete the comparisons between the two couples as in the example.

slightly	nearly	much/far
about	twice	as much as
more/less/fewer	half	considerably
exactly	five times	as many as
a great deal	over	

	MARTIN	FIONA	RUPERT	RACHEL
Age	39	42	37	29
Height	1m 77cm	1m 68cm	1m 76cm	1m 65cm
Weight	96kg	48kg	75kg	59kg
Working day	9 hrs	5.5 hrs	6 hrs	3 hrs
Annual income	£42,000	£16,500	£32,000	£8,000
Exercise per week	1 hr	2 hrs	4 hrs	1.5 hrs

1 (AGE) Rachel *is considerably younger than* Fiona.
2 (AGE) Martin is .... Rupert.
3 (WEIGHT) Fiona weighs .... Martin.
4 (WEIGHT) Martin weighs .... Rupert.
5 (HEIGHT) Rupert is .... Martin.
6 (HEIGHT) Fiona is .... Rachel.
7 (WORK) Martin works .... Rachel.
8 (WORK) Fiona works .... Rupert.
9 (INCOME) Rachel earns .... Fiona.
10 (INCOME) Martin earns .... Rachel.
11 (EXERCISE) Rupert takes .... Martin.
12 (EXERCISE) Rachel takes .... Fiona.

5 Linking and logical devices – addition, concession, contrast

Complete the following sentences with suitable linking devices. An asterisk (*) indicates at least two possible answers. Look at the example.

1 Jenny speaks *both/not only* Russian *and/but also* excellent Chinese.
2 .... does Jenny speak Russian, ... excellent Chinese.
3 Jenny speaks Russian. *...................... , she speaks excellent Chinese.
4 *...................... speaking Russian, Jenny speaks excellent Chinese.
5 They looked at us *...................... we came from another planet!
6 *...................... the doctor told him to rest for a week, he was back at work after two days.
7 .... we'd caught the earlier train we wouldn't have got there on time. So, stop worrying!
8 I know she's a sensible girl and .... I can't help worrying about her.
9 They played golf all morning *...................... the torrential rain.
10 We thought it was going to be a great match. .... , it turned out to be rather dull.
11 They've got no chance of winning the game; .... , they're training every day.
12 Some people like boxing, *...................... others absolutely detest it.

STUDY TIP   *even if* vs *even though*

► Remember that *even if* is used before statements that are hypothetical i.e. not fact:
e.g. Even if I had all the money in the world, I wouldn't buy that car.
We wouldn't have caught the plane even if we'd taken a taxi.
► *Even though*, on the other hand, is used before statements that are fact:
e.g. She's not happy with her job even though she's just had a pay rise and promotion.
He went to the cinema with his friends even though he'd already seen the film.

6 Spelling

6.2 Here is a quick checklist of the main areas of difficulty:

- silent letter combinations – *know, comb, wrong, castle,* etc.
- doubling consonants to maintain correct pronunciation – *taped* (past of *tape*) vs *tapped* (past of *tap*), *cuter* (from *cute*) vs *cutter* (from *cut*), etc.
- doubling consonant on stressed final syllable before a suffix:

  ○ ○   ○ ○ ○   ○ **0**   ○ **0** ○
  differ   *differing*   *defer*   *deferring*

  0 ○ ○   **0** ○ ○ ○   ○ **0**   ○ **0** ○
  benefit   *benefited*   *admit*   *admitted*

- doubling final 'l' after no more than one vowel – *travel > travelled, control > controller,* vs *reveal > revealed*
- dropping final 'e' before suffixes starting with a vowel – *write > writing* (but *age > aging* or *ageing*), *create > creating, collapse > collapsible, collaborate > collaboration*
- final 'y' changes to 'i' only if preceded by a consonant and followed by a suffix not beginning with 'i' – *try > tried* vs *trying*
- negative prefixes before specific letters – *im + p (impolite), il + l (illogical), ir + r (irresponsible)*
- differences between GB and US English – *colour* vs *color, traveller* vs *traveler*
- individual oddities!

6.2 Now check the following sentences. Correct any spelling mistakes you find.

1 They stoped the car to ask the way.
2 The police are patroling this area more and more.
3 We are studing the fall of the Roman Empire at the moment.
4 It is debateable whether the death penalty is an effective deterrent.
5 I keep forgeting where I've left my keys.
6 I remember we stayed in a lovely guesthouse near the centre of town.
7 Jane seems much happyer now that she's living on her own.
8 Unfortunately, Frank panicked and crashed the car.
9 The college provides residential accomodation for all its students.
10 It's doutful whether they'll get beyond the semi-finals.

7 Emphasisers

Some of the emphasisers placed before the adjectives in the sentences below have been used incorrectly. Make any necessary corrections. Look at the example given.

1 The old castle is an ~~absolutely~~ *extremely* attractive place to visit at sunset.
2 Oh, I'm awfully sorry, I didn't see you sitting there.
3 By the time we got home we were very exhausted and went straight to bed.
4 Jack was truly angry about not getting the promotion he wanted.
5 You said there was some petrol in the car but it was completely empty.
6 I wish I'd brought my umbrella. We're going to get extremely soaked in this rain.
7 We were totally happy to hear that you've passed all your exams.
8 The way Luisa can switch between three languages is very impressive.
9 Most people found the documentary deeply shocking.
10 I'll never forget that tremendously delicious meal we had on the last day of our holiday.

8 Review writing

For questions 1–15 read the film review below and then decide which word best fits in each space. The exercise begins with an example (0).

Having seen the (0) ..*trailer*.. on TV for this latest Sam Spadacci film, I knew I was in for something a little different! The main (1) .... of the film (2) .... with the fall and eventual rise of Frankie Longo, (3) .... by the new Hollywood superstar Larry Zardini. The (4) ...., which has some brilliant one-liners, was written by Spadacci's old associate, Matt Dusi.

Everything starts off fairly predictably – a young Italo-American kid, mixed up with the local Mafia – it seems to be the usual (5) .... of Spadacci's own roots. But then, after going in and out of jail for a couple of years, Frankie 'gets cuisine' and suddenly discovers he's a marvellous cook! Some (6) .... are a little slow-moving as we (7) .... on Frank's culinary prowess – did we really need to spend five minutes of the film watching Frank's perfect soufflé rising in the oven?

Soon Frankie is cooking for the rich and famous, including the Mafia big cheese Joe d'Ancona – a wonderfully over the top (8) .... by veteran Bruno Marmo – and eventually the President! Inevitably, in (9) .... of his efforts to go straight, Frankie is caught up in a secret (10) .... to assassinate the President. Without giving too much away, Frankie apparently goes along with the Mafia while really sabotaging things. There are some crazy (11) ...., including gangsters exploding out of a giant birthday cake! The (12) .... maintains the almost slapstick feel with a manic tempo at times.

(13) .... some of the dialogue is a little laboured at times this is, all in (14) ...., a thoroughly entertaining bit of fun, which I (15) .... whole-heartedly.

0	A commercial	B episode	C trailer	D broadcast
1	A storyline	B narrative	C contents	D commentary
2	A concerns	B shows	C describes	D deals
3	A designed	B set	C played	D cast
4	A chapter	B script	C speech	D story
5	A study	B survey	C test	D revision
6	A sections	B chapters	C acts	D scenes
7	A analyse	B focus	C devote	D examine
8	A character	B part	C performance	D personality
9	A spite	B account	C despite	D view
10	A plot	B design	C agreement	D intention
11	A stages	B stunts	C actions	D productions
12	A beat	B singing	C record	D soundtrack
13	A While	B Except	C Although	D Whereas
14	A balance	B all	C conclusion	D end
15	A offer	B suggest	C recommend	D represent

7 ▶ The Ages of Man

1 Grammar

1.1 used to ... vs be/get used to ... ▶ Study Box, SB page 102

Match the first half of each short dialogue (1–10) with its corresponding second half (A–J) and then complete them with a suitable form of *used to ...* or *be/get used to ...* . The exercise starts with an example.

1 Oh dear. I've never driven such a powerful car before. `E`
2 Don't you play tennis? ☐
3 It must be really hard to get up at five every morning. ☐
4 I hear Roger was really shocked when he first started work for the murder squad. ☐
5 Valeria didn't really know what to do when she went to live on her own. ☐
6 I thought you didn't like opera. ☐
7 I don't think I'll ever understand this new computer program! ☐
8 Why did you give up your job just after the new boss took over? ☐
9 Have you noticed how many people drink bottled mineral water these days? ☐
10 Did Gerry enjoy his time in the army? ☐

A Well, there's no rush. Give yourself a month .... it.
B Oh, not really. I .... it by now.
C I know. She .... waited on hand, foot and finger by her mum.
D Not really. He never could .... orders!
E Don't worry, you'll soon *get used to* it.
F Strange, isn't it? No-one ever .... when I was a lad.
G Well, I .... but I really enjoy it now.
H I just .... under so much pressure.
I Oh, I .... but I haven't practised for ages.
J Yes, but he .... the job in the end.

1.2 Past simple or present perfect? ▶ Focus on Grammar, SB page 102

Using the verbs and any other words given in brackets, complete the following sentences with the most suitable form of either the past simple or the present perfect. An example is given to help you.

1 Maria *saw* (see) the doctor yesterday about that rash she *has had* (have) for ages now.
2 'How long .... you .... (live) in Spain?'
   'Two years altogether, before moving to Italy.'
3 OK. Who .... (take) my best pen? It .... (be) on my desk thirty seconds ago.
4 In the Middle Ages people .... (not live) so long as they do now.
5 Oh dear, what .... (happen) to you? You look as though you .... (see) a ghost!
6 Who .... (write) William Tell? I can never remember if it .... (be) Mozart or Rossini.
7 Where .... you .... (buy) those trousers? They're fantastic!
8 It's definitely our favourite film, we .... (see) it six times.
9 .... you ever .... (steal) apples when you .... (be) a kid?
10 Thomas .... (be) late for every lesson so far.
11 I hear you .... (go) to St Petersburg on your honeymoon. What .... you .... (think) of the place?
12 Hello Julia. When .... you .... (get) here?
13 Ah, madam. I believe you .... (witness) the accident. Could you tell me exactly what .... (happen)?
14 Hugo .... (break) his leg so he can't go skiing next month.
15 Ella .... (smoke) forty cigarettes a day for over thirty years. Then she .... (give up) overnight and .... (not touch) one since!

1.3 Present perfect simple and continuous ▶Focus on Grammar, SB page 102

In the following sentences decide whether to use the present perfect simple, the present perfect continuous or the past simple tense of the verbs in brackets and fill in any other missing words as in the example.

1 How long *have* you *been running* (run) the hotel *for* now?
2 When .... you .... (see) the doctor? I .... (not see) him yet.
3 I .... (learn) Japanese .... about six months now. It's really interesting.
4 How long .... you .... (live) in Japan before coming back to England?
5 .... Rob .... (finish) his novel? Oh yes. It .... just .... (be) published.
6 They .... (live) in that same little house .... the day they .... (get) married 20 years ago. I don't think they'll move now!
7 What a fantastic old car! How long .... you .... (have) it?
8 .... you .... (suffer) from these pains in your chest .... a long time?
9 I see they still .... (not repair) that big hole in the road.
10 The team .... (not win) a single match so far this season.
11 Don't we need some groceries? Don't worry, I .... (take) care of that. I .... (do) the shopping on the way home.
12 .... Maisy .... (phone) yet? Yes, about 10 minutes ago. She .... (say) she can't make it tonight.
13 How many of those chocolates .... you .... (eat) so far?
14 We .... (use) my father's garage as a storeroom for our furniture .... the fire. We still .... (not find) anywhere permanent to live.
15 Julie .... (eat) nothing but 'paella' .... her trip to Spain.

1.4 Stative vs dynamic verbs ▶Focus on Grammar, SB page 103

Complete the gaps in the dialogue below using the correct form of the verbs and any other words given in the brackets. See the example.

'Why (1) *are you smelling* (you smell) that cheese, Ted?'
'I (2) .... (think) about eating it, of course.'
'Well, I (3) .... (not think) that's a very good idea. It (4) .... (look) a bit strange and it (5) .... (definitely smell) off!'
'Maybe, but I bet it (6) .... (taste) great.'
'Well, I (7) .... (realise) it's up to you but don't say I didn't warn you.'

(Half an hour later)
'Oooh Donald, I (8) .... (not feel) too well.'
'Well, to be honest, that (9) .... (not surprise) me one little bit. You (10) .... (seem) almost determined to make yourself ill at times. I (11) .... (remember) the time with those oysters!'
'OK, OK. Listen, I (12) .... (need) a rest but I (13) .... (see) Nancy in an hour …'
'And I (14) .... (suppose) you'd like me to put her off.'
'Thanks Dougal, and I (15) .... (promise) I'll listen to you in the future.'

2 Dictionary skills

In all of the following exercises you should use a good monolingual dictionary to help you find the answers.

2.1 Connotation

In the following sentences, decide on the different meanings of the underlined words and if they are being used to give a positive, negative or neutral connotation.

1 Phil has got incredibly underlined hairy forearms, hasn't he?
2 It was rather underlined hairy coming down the mountain road with no lights on the car.
3 Anna's really underlined funny, she just makes me laugh and laugh.
4 I thought there was something a bit underlined funny about his explanation of the accident.
5 In spite of the forecast, it turned out to be a underlined fine day.
6 As a restorer of old paintings, she must have an eye for underlined fine detail.

2.2 Parts of speech

Decide the grammatical function of each of the underlined words.

7 The <u>poor</u> are always with us.
8 Sorry, I'm afraid I explained that rather <u>poorly</u>.
9 Many students are quite <u>poor</u>.
10 Jack's feeling rather <u>poorly</u> so he's staying at home today.

2.3 Metaphors and Idioms

Which of the following words can come after the word *hard* and what do they mean? (four do not exist)

11 headed	12 luck	13 up	14 brained
15 nut	16 eared	17 sleeper	18 drink
19 cash	20 hearted		

2.4 Collocation

Match the verbs in Column A with the correct parts of the body in Column B and try doing the actions! With five of the verbs it is not really necessary to add the part of the body – which are they?

A		**B**	
21	wink	A	your lips
22	snap	B	your head
23	nod	C	your eyelashes
24	shrug	D	your thumbs
25	flutter	E	your nose
26	twiddle	F	your hands
27	pick	G	your eye
28	clench	H	your shoulders
29	pout	I	your fingers
30	clap	J	your fist

2.5 Word formation (derivations)

Use the correct form of the word *use* in each sentence.

31 Haven't you got another dictionary? This one's absolutely .... !
32 The computer disks got wet so they were no longer ....
33 Before buying a .... car, it's a good idea to have it checked by a mechanic.

34 I think your time could be more .... spent than reading comics all day.
35 .... of the photocopier are kindly requested to report any breakdowns to the secretary.

2.6 Pronunciation and stress

For words 36 to 40 cross out the silent letters. For 41 to 45, draw bubbles to show the correct stress, e.g. correct.

36 buoy	37 wrestling	38 knick-knack
39 comb	40 sword	41 guitar
42 photographer	43 difficulty	44 calculator
45 original		

3 Reported speech

▶ Focus on Grammar, SB page 105

Put the following sentences into reported speech. Pay particular attention to the type of reporting verb (avoid *said*). The first one has been done for you.

1 'That's correct. The new ringroad will be built through the wood.'
The government official confirmed that the new ringroad would be built through the wood.

2 'Don't worry. I'll repair the back door this weekend'.
Colin ....

3 'Alright, it's true. It was me who scratched the car.'
Karen ....

4 'If you don't give me £5,000, I'm going to tell the police all about it.'
Maurice ....

5 'You must come to Dave's party with me on Saturday.'
Hilary ....

6 'Oh, by the way, Terry's house is still for sale.'
Silvia ....

7 'Honest to God, I've never seen this money before in my life.'
Mr Penfold ....

8 'Don't go walking in the fog, it can be very dangerous.'
The mountain guide ....

9 'Oh, just a minute, was it Leonardo or Michelangelo who painted the Mona Lisa?'
He couldn't ....

10 'Well, I'd like you all to know Nina and I are getting married next year.'
Julian ....

11 'Oh, I'm easily the best tennis player at the college.'
Jemima ....

12 'Would you mind repeating the question, Dr McPherson?'
Dr Bianchi ....

13 'The service in this restaurant is incredibly slow.'
George ....

14 'I think it might be better to wait until the manager gets here.'
The shop assistant ....

15 'Well, Jack, if I were you, I'd eat less and take more exercise.'
The doctor ....

> **STUDY TIP** Reported speech
>
> ▶ When reporting what someone said it is not always necessary to change the tense of what was said if it is still true:
> e.g. 'Don't worry, I'm coming next week,' said Gus.
> Someone reporting this shortly afterwards would say:
> Gus assured us he's coming next week.

4 Expressions with *make*

Make an appropriate question using the verb *make* to produce each of the following answers. Look at the example given.

1 Q: How much does he *make*?
A: About $100,000 a year. He's just been promoted again.

2 Q: What .... ?
A: Let's see … . Just gone three.

3 Q: Do you reckon George .... a good boss?
A: Not really. He's too arrogant.

4 Q: So, why can't you .... this evening?
A: Because I've got to go to a college meeting at eight.

5 Q: What .... ?
A: Um … 138. Is that right?

6 Q: Do you think we .... ?
A: I'm not sure. But we mustn't give up.

5 Discourse cloze

Read through the following text and choose from the list A–J the best phrase to fit each space. Some of the suggested answers do not fit at all. The exercise begins with an example (0).

The Roots of Discipline

Humour is strong and flexible. Tragedy is brittle. If we change all our children's misdeeds into tragedy, (0) .J. . If all their mistakes are exposed and judged, as before the High Court, they will swiftly feel themselves to be victims of an unyielding system. Soon they feel that not only what they did was bad, (1) .... .

But if a child can make mistakes in safety, (2) .... , or through laughter, his trust and feeling of parental acceptance is not destroyed. The lesson will, however, still be learned. Humour defuses a situation; (3) .... .

Quite simply, the best way to convey discipline to our children is to discipline ourselves. We are the signposts to our children's futures, (4) .... .

It makes sense to take responsibility for our own actions, and respect and accept our own feelings (5) .... . We are then less likely to hide behind a liberal or an authoritarian mask that is unable to reflect the full range of our feelings.

A and they are always looking to us to see where to go
B if we wish to develop as human beings
C but that they are intrinsically bad, too
D as we travel through life together
E but also that their parents are totally out of control
F learn through the warmth of a cuddle
G seriousness augments it
H which is, of course, its greatest strength
I before we discipline the child
J they soon learn the unhappiness of existence

6 Wordcheck – Age

Fill in the missing words in the grid below to reveal another hidden word associated with age. Look at the example given.

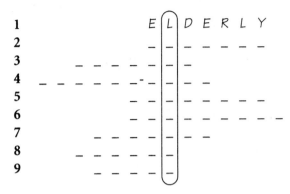

1 Word used to describe old people.
2 Young child who is learning or has just learned to walk.
3 Physical strength to do something over long periods of time.
4 No longer young but not yet old.
5 Someone aged between 13 and 19.
6 If you are aged between 70 and 79 you are in your ....
7 A child with special gifts or great ability.
8 A very young child.
9 If you are 32, you are in your .... thirties.

Personally Speaking

1 Compound adjectives

Word formation, SB page 120

Complete the following sentences with compound adjectives to describe character. The first letters are given to help you. See the example provided.

1 My God! You're so *empty-headed*. How could you leave a broken bottle in the children's play area?
2 Fanny's become really b...............-h............... since she won the tennis tournament!
3 You needn't worry about shocking my parents, they're very b...............-m............... .
4 Emma is terribly t...............-s............... ; she takes offence at the most innocent remarks.
5 Don't bother asking Lisa for a loan, she's really t...............-f............... .
6 If you want some sensible suggestions, go and ask Julia – she's pretty l...............-h............... .
7 Be careful how you treat him, he's so s...............-t............... he's likely to blow up at any moment!

2 *The ... the ...* – comparatives

▶ Study Box, SB page 113

Complete the following sentences with a suitable comparative form. The first one is shown as an example.

1 The *hotter* (hot) the curry, the *better* (good) she likes it!
2 The .... (interesting) the book, the .... (likely) I am to try and finish it in one evening!
3 The .... (easy) a job is to do, the .... (highly) paid are the people who do it.
4 The .... (wine) he drank, the .... (clearly) he spoke.

5 The .... (close) it got to the time of the interview, the .... she became.
6 The .... (humid) it became, the .... (bad) they felt.
7 The .... (far) we climbed up the mountain, the .... the clouds became.
8 .... , the more determined I am to succeed.
9 The less students contribute in class, ...
10 .... , the less fluently one speaks a foreign language.

3 Phrasal verbs

▶ Focus on Vocabulary, SB page 113

Complete the following sentences with a suitable phrasal verb from the box below. Remember to use the correct tense or grammatical structure. The first one has been done for you.

face up to	~~pick out~~	tune in	work out
fall back on	tick off	put down	eke out
steer away from	fight out		

1 Don't forget to *tune in* tomorrow at 8.15 to find out who killed Lady Redfern in the last episode of our Radio Murder Mystery series.
2 When packing, I always make a checklist so I can .... things .... as I put them in the suitcase.
3 I think it would be best if you .... your complaints in a letter addressed to the manager.
4 They'll eventually have to .... the fact that the company is going to be closed down.
5 It is said that Isaac Newton .... the law of gravity after he'd been hit on the head by an apple!
6 I try and .... talking about politics with Steven but he always gets back to it sooner or later.
7 When I was a student, I .... what little money I had by buying only second-hand clothes.
8 There's only one place left and I'm not deciding who should have it. You'll have to .... it .... amongst yourselves.

9 When we both lost our jobs at the same time, it was lucky we had our savings to ....

0 The old lady had no trouble in .... the thief at the identity parade.

4 Grammar

Focus on Grammar, SB page 118

4.1 The Passive

Match up the beginning of each sentence in Column A with its ending in Column B and add a suitable passive verb form in the space provided. The first one is shown as an example.

A

1 In the past, small amounts of cocaine used *to be used*. [G]

2 Salt .... on roads. ☐

3 Central heating .... ☐

4 In the future, many of today's hereditary diseases .... ☐

5 Not so long ago, teeth .... ☐

6 In my grandfather's time, a driving licence .... ☐

7 Undeveloped film .... ☐

8 150 years ago, Gaelic .... ☐

9 'Graded readers' are books in which the language .... ☐

10 Hand gestures .... ☐

11 The world's tropical rainforests .... ☐

12 In India, cows .... ☐

B

A to mean different things in different countries.

B to direct sunlight

C much more widely in Scotland than it is today

D by the Romans.

E so quickly that they may all have gone by 2035!

F when there is snow and ice.

G in the production of Coca-Cola.

H as sacred animals.

I at a post office without having to take a test!

J without any anaesthetic!

K so that learners can read them more easily.

L through genetic engineering.

4.2 Fill in the gaps

Complete the gaps in the following passage by putting the verbs in brackets into an appropriate passive form. You will also have to put any other words in brackets in the correct place. Look at the example given.

Well, last month most of the lambs (1) *were sold* (sell) at the market, although we've still got ten, which (2) .... (probably send) next week. When all the lambs have gone, the sheep (3) .... (take) to another part of the farm. After that, we usually start on the fruit, although the blackcurrants (4) .... (already pick) because it was an early season this year. The plums can't (5) .... (pick) for another three weeks by law as they (6) .... (spray) only seven weeks ago. Of course, they still have (7) .... (gather) by hand, unlike the blackcurrants, which (8) .... (harvest) by machine nowadays. The plums and blackcurrants (9) .... (both make) into jam and preserve. Then we have what's called the 'bag fruit', which is apples and pears. Since the fruit doesn't have to be in good condition (10) .... (make) into cider and perry, it (11) .... (treat) pretty badly. For example, there are no skilled pickers involved, the trees (12) .... (just shake) until the fruit drops to the ground, where it (13) .... (collect) and (14) .... (put) into bags. As you can imagine, handling the bags is a very dirty job as the juice leaks out everywhere. But I hope the whole process (15) .... (automate) before much longer.

4.3 *make/cause*, etc.

Add a suitable ending to each of the following sentences using an infinitive verb form with or without *to*. Look at the example provided.

1 Reading an article about the 'greenhouse effect' *persuaded Gary to travel by bicycle more frequently.*

2 The lack of rain caused most of the plants ....

3 The park-keeper wouldn't let the children ....

4 Driving while under the influence of alcohol causes people ....

5 The TV pictures of the damage caused by the flood made us all ....

6   What the doctor said about lung cancer and heart disease convinced Moyra ....

7   The customs officer asked Boris
....

8   The examination invigilator didn't let anyone
....

9   Living and working in a foreign country usually forces you ....

10 Having to deal with tiresome bureaucracy makes me
....

STUDY TIP | *make*

▶ Remember that when *make* is used passively it takes *to* before a following verb:
e.g. They made her leave the room.
She was made to leave the room.

---

5 Writing – Informal letter

Use the following notes to write a letter of invitation to a friend. You must use all the words in the same order as the notes. You may add words and change the form of words where necessary but do not add any extra information. The first one has been done for you.

1 many thanks postcard Greece – get last week.

2 glad hear have good time – apart sunburn!

3 hope get over it – feel better now.

4 anyway reason write – Kim and I party Saturday 19th celebrate end exams.

5 know rather long way come but wonder you like stay weekend.

6 both hope able make it.

7 can let know come by next Friday?

8 Hope hear soon

Dear Sam,
1   *Many thanks for your postcard from Greece, which we got last week.*

2   ....

3   ....

4   ....

5   ....

6   ....

7   ....

8   ....

All the best,

STUDY TIP | Informal letters

▶ Remember the following points when writing an informal letter:

DO	DON'T
write the salutation (e.g. *Dear Sally*) against the left hand margin.	begin *Dear Friend*
begin the first paragraph under the first letter of the correspondent's name.	
indent the following paragraphs slightly in from the left hand margin.	
end with *Best wishes* or *Love* (depending on how well you know the person).	use the formal endings *Yours sincerely/faithfully.*

---

6 Wordcheck – Character and personality

In each of the following groups of words there is one that doesn't fit. <u>Underline</u> the odd word out. The first one has been done for you.

1 critical	defensive	sarcastic	<u>persistent</u>
2 keen	restless	eager	ambitious
3 harsh	unfeeling	impatient	insensitive
4 diligent	talkative	friendly	chatty
5 shy	withdrawn	timid	calm
6 carefree	attentive	careful	cautious
7 happy	content	cheerful	charming
8 trustworthy	dynamic	reliable	dependable

7 Lexical cloze

Read the following text carefully and choose the answer which best fits each space. The first answer has been given as an example.

Smile Power

The expression on your face can actually dramatically (0) B.. your feelings and perceptions, and it has been proved that (1) .... smiling or frowning can create corresponding emotional responses. The idea was first (2) .... by a French physiologist, Israel Waynbaum, in 1906. He believed that different facial (3) .... affected the flow of blood to the brain, and that this could create positive or negative feelings. A happy smile or irrepressible (4) .... increased the blood flow and contributed to joyful feelings. But sad, angry expressions decreased the flow of oxygen-carrying blood, and created a vicious (5) .... of gloom and depression by effectively (6) .... the brain of essential fuel.

Psychologist Robert Zajonc rediscovered this early (7) .... , and (8) .... that the temperature of the brain could affect the production and synthesis of neurotransmitters – which definitely influence our moods and energy levels. He argues that an impaired blood flow could not (9) .... deprive the brain of oxygen, but create further chemical imbalance (10) .... inhibiting these vital hormonal messages. Zajonc goes on to propose that our brains remember that smiling is associated with being happy, and that by deliberately smiling through your tears you can (11) .... your brain to release uplifting neurotransmitters – replacing a depressed condition (12) .... a happier one. People suffering from psychosomatic (13) .... , depression and anxiety states could (14) .... from simply exercising their zygomatic (15) .... – which pull the corners of the mouth up and back to form a smile – several times an hour.

0	A effect	B alter	C arrange	D reduce
1	A desperately	B determinedly	C deliberately	D decidedly
2	A put off	B put down	C put by	D put forward
3	A aspects	B looks	C expressions	D appearances
4	A laughter	B sadness	C humour	D depression
5	A cycle	B spiral	C circle	D vortex
6	A cutting	B starving	C removing	D eliminating
7	A result	B subject	C research	D experiment
8	A advises	B wants	C demands	D suggests
9	A even	B only	C ever	D always
10	A by	B without	C when	D from
11	A make	B persuade	C allow	D decide
12	A through	B by	C after	D with
13	A disease	B illness	C infection	D ailment
14	A recover	B improve	C benefit	D progress
15	A muscles	B nerves	C veins	D bones

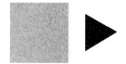

Progress Test Two

Units 5–8

1 Structural cloze

For questions 1–15, complete the following story by writing each missing word in the space.
Use only one word for each space. The exercise begins with an example (0).

A summer job

'Oh good, you're here at last. I was wondering what time you'd (0) *arrive*,' snapped the boss. 'I've been waiting for you (1) .... three quarters of an hour!'

I apologised and explained that the early morning traffic had been (2).................... heavier than I'd expected.

'Oh dear! I don't suppose you're (3) .... to getting up so early after your time at university. To be honest, I'm surprised you were (4) .... to get here before midday,' he added sarcastically. I smiled and said nothing.

The job was driving a bus around Stratford (5) .... Cheryl, the boss's daughter, gave a description of the places of interest we were passing.

We set off at half past nine with a bus full of tourists. Suddenly Cheryl hissed into my ear, 'How (6) .... have you had your licence? You drive (7) .... a complete lunatic! Slow down or they won't see anything.'

'Sorry,' I said, gritting my teeth. 'I'll (8) .... my best.'

At 11 o'clock, the tourists and Cheryl went into Anne Hathaway's cottage so I decided to go and have a cup of coffee. The cafe was a (9) .... further away than I realised and I had to stand in the queue for ages – it (10) .... have taken me 20 minutes to get served. When I got back to the bus, Cheryl was furious.

'Where on earth have you (11) .... ?' shouted Cheryl.

'I just went for a coffee. Your father said it (12) .... be OK,' I protested.

When we got back, Cheryl told her father about my dreadful behaviour. But before he (13) .... to open his mouth, I said 'Look, I've had just about enough of this. Don't bother to sack me, I won't be (14) .... in tomorrow!' and walked out.

I later found out that they had had four different drivers in (15) .... many weeks.

---

2 Phrasal verbs

Complete each of the following sentences with the appropriate form of a suitable phrasal verb. An example sentence is provided.

Example: Hal had no trouble in *calling up* all the data we needed on the computer screen.

1 Giving up my job to go and live abroad .... to be the biggest mistake I've ever made.

2 Jane has always .... her brother even when he was accused of murder and everyone else refused to speak to him.

3 This watch used to belong to my great-great-grandfather. It's been .... from father to son for five generations.

4 My karate instructor always .... Robert to demonstrate techniques as he's the best in the class.

5 I've got to drive, so I think I'd better .... orange juice, thanks all the same.

3 Word formation

Read the texts below. Use the words in the box to form one word that fits in the numbered space in the texts. The exercise begins with an example (0).

From what we had read in the (0) *advertisement*, it promised to be the holiday of a lifetime – not only a quality hotel in a top (1) .... resort, but also (2) .... cheap with it! We should have known it was too good to be true! We arrived at the airport to discover we only had (3) .... tickets and there was no guarantee we would be flying. Luckily, two places became free at the last minute and we took off. The flight lasted at least (4) .... as long as it should have and by the time we arrived, we were both feeling rather (5) .... , probably because of the dubious in-flight meal we had had. We were met by our guide, who seemed (6) .... incompetent and understood very little of what we said to him. Instead of the hotel we had seen in the photograph back home, he took us to a squalid little guesthouse much (7) .... away from the resort than we were expecting. We wanted to explain that there had been a dreadful mistake but it was (8) .... trying to complain – nobody could understand us!

How to be sensitive

When asked to talk about themselves, some people, particularly men, become rather (9) .... Others become (10) .... , unable to sit still or look at their inquisitor. Others, however, become extremely (11) .... , delighted to have been given the opportunity to talk about themselves. Jenny falls into this latter category. One innocent question about her health can result in half an hour's in-(12) .... description of her backache or sleepless night. What's more, you daren't interrupt her for fear of offending her legendary (13) .... and being described as an (14) .... egotist with no interest in other people! I have now learned that all (15) .... is futile and one simply has to grin and bear it.

0	ADVERTISE
1	SEA
2	SURPRISE
3	STAND
4	TWO
5	POOR
6	LANGUAGE
7	FAR
8	USE

9	DEFEND
10	REST
11	TALK
12	DEEP
13	SENSE
14	FEEL
15	RESIST

4 Register cloze

Read the following information sheet about hiring a car while on holiday in Greece and use the information to complete the numbered gaps in the informal letter to a friend. Use no more than two words for each gap. The words you need do not occur in the information sheet. The exercise begins with an example (0).

GENERAL CAR HIRE CONDITIONS

1 Cars should be booked at the same time as your holiday. If added later, a fax or telex fee may be incurred.

2 A small charge (c. £5 per day) to offset extra insurance costs is made for additional drivers and payable locally.

3 Drivers must be at least 23 years of age for Groups A, B and C, 25 years of age for other Groups, and have held a full UK driving licence for 12 months. All drivers should be entered individually on the contract to be completed when collecting the car – you will need passport, driving licence, 'Hellas' voucher and a credit card.

4 Damage to the tyres, engine or underside of the car is not covered by insurance in Greece. A credit card imprint or cash deposit of approximately £100 will be required on delivery of the car, returnable at the end of the hire period on condition that the car is returned with no damage to the above.

5 Outside normal office hours (0800–2000) an out-of-hours delivery charge is payable locally, normally c. £15.

6 Child seats and roof racks are available on request only and at a charge of c. £3 per day payable locally.

7 Cars may be booked for periods of less than 7 days but the daily rate increases – please telephone us for a quote. Car hire prices are calculated on 24 hour periods.

Dear Fabienne,

Sorry it's taken me so long to get back in touch but I've been up to my eyes in work. Anyway, I did manage to find out about hiring a car if you book your holiday with 'Hellas'. The first thing is to book the car when you pay for your holiday or there'll be some extra (0) *charges*. If David's going to drive (1) .... , you'll have to pay another £5 a day. I know you're both (2) .... twenty-three but have you both (3) .... for more than 12 months? If you haven't, you won't be allowed to drive! Also, don't forget to (4) .... both your names on the contract you sign in Greece. They'll also ask you for a deposit for (5) .... £100 to (6) .... any damage you might do to the car. But don't worry, you'll (7) .... this back so long as you bring the car back in one (8) .... ! Child seats don't come as standard, so you'll have to (9) .... one for little Rory when you're there. It'll (10) .... you another £3 a day.

5 Lexical cloze

Read the following text carefully and choose the answer which best fits each space. The first answer has been given as an example (0).

Stress-related hair loss

When stress levels become so high that they affect the immune system it can have a (0) *C.* effect on the body and the hair. Hair loss itself causes immense stress and then it can become a vicious (1) .... .

Bonnie Kinnear, 50s, housewife: 'Last year my life was quite stressful due to my husband's high-profile career being constantly in the (2) .... . At this time I began to develop an (3) .... scalp which was wrongly diagnosed as psoriasis, for which I was (4) .... steroids. Over the next two months my scalp became worse, and hair began to fall out, leaving (5) .... patches, which was devastating.

Having to look good and be a support to my famous husband was stressful because wherever we went people would look at us. I had lost at (6) .... one third of my hair and, in (7) .... , visited a high-profile Mayfair trichologist. Without any (8) .... I was ordered to buy £300 (9) .... of products and my head was massaged by a girl who proceeded to turn my hair into what is (10) .... as 'bird's-nest syndrome'. It took four hours to (11) .... .

My GP (12) .... me to seek help from Andrew Bernie. I was diagnosed with a stress-triggered (13) .... where the skin cells multiply fast, grow down the hairshaft and bind with sebaceous matter to strangle the hair. I visit Andrew regularly for (14) .... . I am also trying to (15) .... my stress levels, which is easier now my hair is returning.

0	A hard	B heavy	C profound	D full
1	A cycle	B effect	C closure	D circle
2	A daylight	B spotlight	C searchlight	D starlight
3	A intense	B enlarged	C inflamed	D inflicted
4	A prescribed	B ordered	C allowed	D recommended
5	A empty	B bald	C dark	D hairy
6	A once	B all	C least	D first
7	A reply	B fun	C hope	D desperation
8	A experiment	B diagnosis	C study	D result
9	A worth	B value	C price	D cost
10	A supposed	B known	C seen	D referred
11	A replace	B untangle	C return	D reset
12	A suggested	B forbade	C convinced	D reported
13	A state	B symptom	C outcome	D condition
14	A treatments	B dates	C services	D appointments
15	A destroy	B assess	C manage	D measure

6 Discourse cloze

For questions 1–6, read through the following text and then choose from the list A–J the best phrase or sentence to fill each of the spaces. Write one letter (A–J) in the correct space. Some of the answers do not fit at all. The exercise begins with an example (0).

Indo-European Languages

Today, most European languages, and many Asian languages as far east as India, are very similar to each other. (0) *J.* about memorising French word lists in school, these so-called 'Indo-European' languages resemble English and each other in terms of vocabulary and grammar (1) .... . Only 140 of the modern world's 5,000 tongues belong to this language family, (2) .... . Thanks to the global expansion of Europeans since 1492 – especially people from England, Spain, Portugal, France and Russia – nearly half the world's present population of five billion now speaks an Indo-European language as its native tongue.

When, however, we go to parts of the world (3) .... , we realise how unusual Europe's linguistic similarity is, and how it calls for explanation. (4) .... , in areas of the New Guinea highlands (5) .... , we find languages as different as English is from Chinese being spoken in neighbouring areas. (6) .... until some people speaking the mother tongue of the Indo-European language family began to dominate and pushed almost all other European languages out of existence.

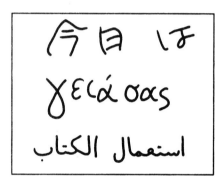

A   as well as French
B   Eurasia must have originally been as diverse
C   For example
D   which must have originated outside Europe
E   yet differ in this respect from all the world's other languages
F   In spite of this
G   where contact with the outside world began only in the 20th century
H   but their importance is far out of proportion to their numbers
I   with great linguistic diversity
J   No matter how much we complain

9 ▶ # Mind Your Manners

1 Inversion after negative introductions

Study Box, SB page 127

Complete the following sentences to make a more dramatic version of the sentence printed above it. The first one has been done for you.

1 You mustn't press this red button under any circumstances.
   Under no circumstances must you press this red button.

2 She'd only just stubbed out one cigarette when she lit another.
   Hardly ....

3 We didn't see a soul all day.
   Not ....

4 As soon as I put the phone down, it rang again!
   No sooner ....

5 He spoke so quietly that I didn't hear a thing he said.
   So ....

6 They didn't win a game all season.
   Not ....

7 Life is like that.
   Such ....

8 She didn't realise who he was until she'd been speaking to him for ten minutes.
   Only after ....

9 Kate not only spilled wine on the carpet but she also broke six glasses.
   Not only ....

10 I'd never seen such a gigantic fish before!
   Never .... !

2 Modal verbs

▶ Focus on Grammar, SB page 128

Complete the following sentences using a suitable modal verb to express obligation or permission together with the verb in brackets. The first one is shown as an example.

1 You *must go* (go) and see that new play at the Adelphi. It's marvellous!

2 Guests .... (leave) their valuables in the hotel safe if they wish.

3 It was lucky we .... (change) any money as all the banks were shut.

4 We .... (rush) after all. The plane was over an hour late taking off.

5 You .... (have) a special licence to drive lorries weighing over two tons.

6 Sorry to interrupt, Professor Cripwell. .... I .... (ask) you a quick question?

7 In the future, European citizens .... (travel) from one country to another inside Europe without going through customs.

8 We really .... (have) the car washed. It's absolutely filthy!

9 I've no idea where the inn is. So when we get to the village, we .... (ask) for directions.

10 Unlike many other countries, young men in Britain .... (do) compulsory military service as it was abolished in 1957.

11 You used .... (build) a house more or less anywhere on your land 100 years ago. Today you .... (put) a shed in your garden without planning permission!

12 .... we .... (discuss) this any further? I'm sure we've all got a good idea of the problem now.

13 You .... (keep) the receipt. They won't take it back without one now.

14 I hope we .... (build) an extension on the back of our house next year.

15 At my last job, we .... (make) any personal phone calls from the office. We .... (use) the public call box in the street!

3 Collocations

▶ **Focus on Vocabulary, SB page 130**

3.1 Collocations – verb + noun

Complete the following sentences to make common word partnerships, or collocations. The first one has been done for you.

1 William *takes himself* rather *seriously*, I'm afraid.
2 The government broke their .... not to put up taxes.
3 The town council plans to .... a public meeting to discuss the new car park.
4 Thomas wasted a lot of money on ineffectual advertisements but, in the end, he just put it down to ....
5 Kevin's always cracking terrible .... that only he laughs at!
6 A break from the everyday routine .... everyone a lot of good.
7 Laura raised an interesting .... at the staff meeting yesterday.
8 Jo was asked to .... an explanation for her extraordinary behaviour.
9 The doctor tried to put me at my .... about the operation but I couldn't help being worried.
10 The consultant advised us to bring our computer system up to .... , describing what we've got as antiquated and practically obsolete!
11 The manager told us to give .... to the publicity campaign as that was the most important thing to get finished.
12 She was trying to .... him a compliment but it came out all wrong.
13 Amanda .... an excuse about visiting a sick friend but I don't think she really wanted to come.
14 I made a real .... when I asked her about her husband. How was I to know they'd just split up?
15 It was getting very late but nobody seemed to want to make a .... to break up the party.

3.2 Collocations – verb + adverb

Complete the following sentences with a suitable adverb. See the example.

1 Everyone welcomed us so *warmly* we felt like royalty!
2 He must have said something absolutely hilarious because everyone was laughing up................ .
3 Kimiko cat................ denied having stolen the money.
4 She also de................ resented the fact that I thought she might have done.
5 I later apologised pr................ when it came to light that the money had simply been misplaced.
6 We complained bi................ about the noise outside our bedroom window but nothing was done about it.
7 You're absolutely right. I agree with you whole-................ .
8 I bi................ regret not going to Brazil when I had the chance.
9 We congratulated them wa................ on their wonderful achievement.
10 I'm sorry but I fl................ refuse to do such a stupid thing!

3.3 Collocations – adjective + noun

Match each adjective in the first box with its corresponding noun in the second box and form common collocations to complete the sentences that follow. See the example provided.

ADJECTIVE	family	kind	~~working~~
social	warm	wedding	close
fond	distant	sunny	firm
candle-lit	unkind	relaxed	prior

NOUN	~~lunch~~	welcome	atmosphere
dinner	handshake	engagement	smile
remark	get-together	invitation	friend
climber	farewell	relative	reception

1 I didn't enjoy my meal very much as it was a *working lunch.*
2 Regretfully, we will be unable to attend the Reunion Dinner due to a ....
3 Thank you so much for your .... We'd love to come.

4 Fred is rather two-faced – he's always got some
.... to make about his so-called friends.

5 Apparently, the famous composer William Walton is a
.... of Richard's, although they've never met.

6 And now ladies and gentleman would you please
give a very .... to our next guest, Mr
Danny Muller!

7 I'm dreading it. I'm best man and I've got to make a
humorous speech at the ....

8 Vincent is a terrible .... He's always trying
to get himself invited to the most exclusive parties.

9 As they parted they whispered a .... ,
knowing they would never meet again.

10 I always try and greet business contacts with a
.... and a .... !

11 My mother's birthday is a chance for us all to meet
up and have a ....

12 I'd rather you didn't speak like that about Rachel,
she happens to be a .... of mine.

13 I love going round to Roddy's – there's always such a
....

14 Gerry proposed to Amanda halfway through a
romantic ....

dis-	il-	im-	in-	ir-	mis-	non-	un-

1	formal	*informal*
2	mobile	....
3	rational	....
4	comfortable	....
5	smoker	....
6	relevant	....
7	reliable	....
8	respect	....
9	soluble	....
10	behave	....
11	logical	....
12	comfort	....
13	spell	....
14	polite	....
15	legible	....
16	resident	....

STUDY TIP   Negative prefixes

► Record in groups those words that start with the same negative prefix:
e.g. (verbs) misbehave, misinform, mislay
(adjectives) misguided, misnamed
► Remember that certain prefixes occur before certain spellings:
e.g. il- (illogical, illiterate) – usually before a word beginning with l
im- (impersonal, immature) – usually before a word beginning with m or p
ir- (irrational, irreparable) – usually before a word beginning with r

STUDY TIP   Collocations

► It is very important to know which words frequently go together to form collocations (word partnerships). A good idea to help build up your knowledge of collocations is to create 'key word grids':
e.g.

verbs	describing words	key word	words that come after
catch	wrong		stop
miss	last	BUS	pass
get on	crowded		fare
stop	night		station

Try to make your own grids with common key words.

4 Dictionary skills

In each of the following exercises you should use a good English/English dictionary to help you find the answers.

4.1 Opposites – prefixes

Find the opposites for the following words using the prefixes in the box. The first one has been done for you.

4.2 Synonyms and antonyms

Write a (near) synonym and antonym for each of the following adjectives.

		SYNONYM	ANTONYM
17	cheeky	....	....
18	brainy	....	....
19	skinny	....	....
20	handy	....	....

<table>
<tr><td>STUDY TIP</td><td>Phonetics</td></tr>
</table>

▶ Some phonetic symbols are quite easy to understand e.g. /k/, /z/, /p/ but there are a few which need to be learnt. Do you know what sounds these symbols represent? If not, check in a dictionary.
/ɔ:/, /θ/, /dʒ/, /ð/, /ɜ:/, /tʃ/

4.3 Phonetics

Find the pronunciation key at the beginning or end of your dictionary. Use it to help you match the following words with the vowel sound they contain. Write the correct phonetic symbol in the box after each word.

	words		sounds
1	cut	☐	/u:/
2	caught	☐	/æ/
3	kit	☐	/ɔ:/
4	cat	☐	/ɜ:/
5	cot	☐	/ɑ:/
6	curt	☐	/ʌ/
7	coot	☐	/ɪ/
8	cart	☐	/ɒ/

4.4 Spelling vs pronunciation

Similar spelling does not always mean similar pronunciation in English. Decide if the following pairs of words have the same vowel sound. Write S (same) or D (different) in the box.

9	bomb	comb	☐
10	low	tow	☐
11	weight	eight	☐
12	stove	glove	☐
13	pour	sour	☐
14	laughter	daughter	☐
15	food	mood	☐
16	rear	pear	☐
17	none	done	☐
18	mown	town	☐

4.5 Pronunciation

The combination of letters 'ough' can be pronounced in seven different ways in English. Put the words in the box below in the correct list depending on the pronunciation of 'ough'.

nought	through	trough	rough
thorough	though	tough	borough
enough	bough	drought	thought
cough	plough	dough	

e.g.	/ʌf/	/ə/	/aʊ/	/əʊ/
	bl<u>uff</u>	<u>a</u>gain	h<u>ow</u>	n<u>o</u>
	....	....	....	....
	....	....	....	....
	....	....	....	....
	/ɔ:/	/ɒf/	/u:/	
	s<u>aw</u>	c<u>o</u>ffee	t<u>oo</u>	
	....	....	....	
	....	....	....	
	....	....	....	

5 Type 3 and mixed conditionals

Re-write the following sentences so that they mean the same as the sentences before them. An example is given.

1 We couldn't have a picnic because it started raining.
 If it hadn't started raining, we could have had a picnic.
2 Jane doesn't live anywhere near London so she didn't apply for that job in the City.
 Jane would ....
3 I only found out because Louis mentioned it to me in passing.
 If Louis ....
4 Ronald is in prison because a detective recognised him from an identikit picture.
 If a detective ....
5 Harry beat me at tennis – but only because he's such a terrible cheat!
 Harry wouldn't ....
6 You left the map in the car – that's why we're lost!
 If you ....
7 We know nothing about engines, so we weren't able to fix the car when it broke down.
 We might ....
8 I didn't prepare anything special because I didn't know they were coming.
 I'd ....

Writing – Report writing

You are writing a report for 'Bocia', the manufacturers of the new 'Bambo' pushchair, based on the results of interviews with mothers and fathers all over the country. The aim of the interviews was to find out how good the pushchair is. Expand the following notes into a full report using the phrases in the box below. You may also use subheadings e.g. Introduction, Observations, Recommendations, etc. Write about 250 words.

> The aim of this report is to ... It is based on ...
> It was found that ... A/The majority/minority of people ...
> In the words of ... On the whole ... It is interesting that ...
> It is recommended that ... It is advisable for 'Bocia' to ...
> 'Bocia' might consider ... To sum up/summarise ... On balance ...

<u>Notes for report on new 'Bambo' pushchair</u>
Number of people interviewed: 150
Interview locations: London, Bristol, Birmingham, Gloucester, Glasgow, Leeds.

<u>Sample comments:</u>
'Compared to our old pushchair, this is fantastic – it's so light and manageable.' Mrs Roberta Long, Gloucester
'My little boy really likes going out in it – so it must be comfy, mustn't it?' Mr Adam Blair, London
'Well, we quite like it but it's a bit stiff to open and close really. That's our only complaint.' Mr and Mrs Osmonth, Leeds
'It folds up really small and fits in the boot of the car no problem. The only thing is it's always getting stuck in little holes.' Mrs Joy McCarthy, Glasgow

<u>Analysis:</u>
Good points
– light
– easy to steer
– good for carrying shopping
– attractive design and colours
– comfortable for baby
– small when folded
– 4 positions for baby, from sitting up to lying flat

Bad points
– difficult to open and close
– wheels too small so it gets stuck in holes on rough ground
– wheels difficult to lock as mechanism is too small to operate by foot

<u>Suggestions (with diagram):</u>

make opening hinge easier to open/close →

→ make wheel locking mechanism larger

increase size of wheels →

7 Register cloze

For questions 1–16, read the following comments from a language school student questionnaire and use the information to complete the numbered gaps in the formal memorandum to staff. Use no more than two words for each gap. The words you need do not occur in the students' comments. The exercise begins with an example (0).

Typical answers to feedback questionnaire:

Classes
'My teacher was late for class every day except the first Monday!'
'I came to England to study English not to play games – I'm not a child!!!'

Facilities
'My classroom (A35) is a mess – can't the repairmen fix the cracks in the walls and stick the wallpaper back on? Only one of the lights was working during the whole 4-week course!'
'I liked the books and things in the self-access centre but it's in a bad place right at the top of the library on the fourth floor! Why not put it somewhere students spend more time?'
'The "Munch House Cafe Bar" is OK – I liked the new chairs and tables. Some of the sandwiches were off and they always ran out of coke when it was hot!'

Food
'I didn't like the food at all – it's always the same – chips, chips, chips!'
'All the food is boring – it has no real taste.'

Activities
'I liked the tour of the city but the sports were terrible, nobody knew where to go or what time to arrive!'
'Tom Shark was very rude to the students and we had to pay for things I thought I'd paid for when I paid for the course – like the BBQs and discos!'

Memorandum

To: All members of EFL staff
From: Jack Boot (Director of Studies)
Date: 16 June
cc: The Principal

RE: STUDENT FEEDBACK QUESTIONNAIRE

I am afraid there were a large number of (0) *complaints* about the school at the end of this course. The following is a summary of the most recurrent comments.

Lessons
(1) .... seems to be a problem with many teachers, in fact one managed to be on time only once during the course. There also seems to be a feeling among students that the lessons weren't (2) .... and that too many games were played in class. Many of our students find such activities rather (3) ....

Facilities
Various students noted that the classrooms are in a (4) .... of repair and that we need to pay greater and more immediate attention to (5) .... As regards the new self-access centre, many students praised the wide selection of (6) .... but commented negatively about its (7) .... at the top of the library building, which, it seems, makes it somewhat (8) .... for students. Another more positive element in the school is the "Munch House". Many students commented favourably about the (9) .... but also pointed out that the sandwiches are often (10) .... and that soft drinks are frequently in short (11) .... particularly during hot weather.

Catering
The food lacks (12) .... with a great deal of the same food appearing day after day. It also seems that the food is far too (13) .... for international students.

Activities
There were numerous negative comments in this area. The sports activities seem very (14) .... organised with students having no clear instructions as to where or when to play. Certain members of the activities staff were also described as (15) .... Finally, it is clear that many students are being charged again for activities they paid for in (16) .... , such as barbecues and discotheques.

I propose to hold an emergency meeting to discuss how best to address the most urgent issues outlined above. The meeting will be this Friday 23 June starting at 4.30pm in the staff room.

All staff are expected to attend.

1 Grammar

1.1 Review of *-ing* forms and infinitives
▶ **Focus on Grammar, SB page 175**

Complete the following sentences with either the infinitive or the *-ing* form of the verb given in brackets. See the example given.

1 *Living* (live) alone is becoming more common nowadays.
2 I'm really looking forward to .... (see) you again next week.
3 Can't we just .... (have) a quiet evening at home for once?
4 It's always difficult .... (know) if and when you should get married.
5 Come on, you kids! Stop .... (shout)! You're driving me crazy.
6 When they split up, Paula made David .... (give) back all the presents she'd ever given him.
7 The most important thing in any relationship is .... (understand) what makes your partner tick.
8 Maurice and Fiona have always let their children .... (do) exactly what they want.
9 With the advances in medical science, it seems that you're never too old .... (have) children any more.
10 When the baby was small I have to admit that I had to wear earplugs at night .... (get) a good night's sleep.

1.2 Cleft sentences and introductory *it*
▶ **Focus on Grammar, SB page 180**

Complete the following dialogues with some form of cleft sentence to give greater emphasis. An example is given to help you.

1 'Didn't George get the sack?'
   'No, the person who got the sack was Jim.'
2 'Aren't you allergic to beans?'
   'No, ... I'm allergic to!' (onions)
3 'I thought you went to Tunisia on your holidays.'
   'Oh come on, I've told you hundreds of times, ... we went to was Turkey!'
4 'How important is a good salary to you?'

'Not very, ... I'm looking for.' (job satisfaction)
5 'I was told Rudy emigrated because he didn't like the weather.'
   'That's just a joke! .... he went away was because he'd been caught stealing credit cards.'
6 'Is that the man you saw breaking into the house?'
   'I don't think so. .... I saw was much taller.'
7 'I'm sure New York was first settled by the British.'
   'That's not right. .... who first settled there and they called it New Amsterdam!'
8 'Did you enjoy yourself at the cinema last night?'
   'Well, unfortunately .... , *Bladerunner*, was sold out. So we went to see some terrible film whose name escapes me.'
9 '............... Shakespeare who wrote the *Canterbury Tales*?'
   'You're joking, aren't you? It was Chaucer, of course!'
10 'Surely English is the most widely spoken language in the world.'
   'Well, actually .... by most people is Mandarin Chinese.'

2 Collocations with *do/make/ have/get*

▶ **Focus on Vocabulary, SB page 181**

Use suitable collocations with *do, make, have* or *get* to complete the sentences below. An example is provided.

1 Now come on, stop crying. *You're making a fuss about nothing.*
2 It's our tenth wedding anniversary and we're going to .... a big .... to celebrate.
3 Neil's never really had a steady girlfriend as he finds it hard to .... a ....
4 Look, I'm sorry about .... we .... last night. I shouldn't have lost my temper and started shouting.
5 Fred and Keiko have just .... and plan to marry next year.
6 I'm pleased to see you've started washing your own clothes at last. But why have I still got to .... the .... ?
7 Sebastian is a really spoilt kid. He always .... his own .... at home.

8 The film was a real 'tear-jerker' and we all sat there at the end .... a good ....

9 Look, we can't have a serious conversation if you're going to be so hysterical. You're just .... no .... at all!

10 Some men still fail to .... their fair .... of the housework.

3 Phrasal verbs

Complete the following dialogue with the correct form of suitable phrasal verbs. See the example.

Jackie: Have you heard the latest?

Lesley: No, what's happened?

Jackie: Well, it seems Emma and Rory have (1) *broken off* their engagement.

Lesley: Really? I must say it doesn't surprise me. They were always (2) .... with each other and then having to kiss and (3) .... They were bound to (4) .... sooner or later.

Jackie: Well, if you ask me, it was more than just arguments. I'm pretty sure Rory was (5) .... her with that 'old friend' of his, Sarah, from university. I heard him (6) .... her .... to the pub with him just the other day and then, surprise, surprise, next morning Emma's complaining that Rory (7) .... her .... for their weekly visit to the cinema!

Lesley: She's better off without him, in my opinion. She's a pretty tough character – she'll soon (8) .... him!

Jackie: Yes. Let's hope she (9) .... someone more sensible next time. They were never really suited. I'm just surprised she didn't (10) .... him sooner – he's such an egotist!

4 Dependent prepositions

Put the correct prepositions in the gaps in the text below. The first one has been done for you.

I must admit that I cringe (1) *at the prospect of going to see my brother.* He is, I suppose, fairly well-read (2) .... his field, which is medicine. However, the way he insists (3) .... always being right all the time, regardless (4) .... how well-informed his conversational adversary may be, makes me quite angry. Whenever anything concerned (5) .... medicine crops up in conversation, he puffs himself up and prepares to 'inform' people. His attitude (6) .... people who get their facts slightly wrong is insufferable. He cannot just let things go, he is just not comfortable (7) .... inaccuracies. It is almost as if he is dropping (8) .... status if he fails to pick someone up on a point. I remember him once arguing with a dinner guest for over an hour on the difference (9) .... the hard and soft palate! No wonder his wife is always complaining (10) .... him!

5 Writing – Information sheet

You have been asked to design an eye-catching information leaflet about the dangers of household poisons to children. Using the information below, create your leaflet. Remember to use main headings and sub-headings; to break up the text in order to avoid blocks; to use visuals e.g. blobs, numbers, asterisks, etc, different styles and sizes of writing, underlining, different colours, boxes and arrows.

Hundreds of children are taken to hospital every year with symptoms of poisoning. Most common causes are household products (for kids tablets = sweets, bottle of bleach = lemonade, a paint brush covered in paint = an ice lolly, rat poison = talcum powder) and plants and berries in the garden.

Parents must be alert at all times – NB keep all medicines locked in cabinets or out of children's reach, fit safety catches to cupboards where cleaning products are stored; teach kids not to drink from bottles or eat brightly coloured berries in the garden.

If you think your child has been poisoned, act quickly – don't wait and see what happens! Don't make your child vomit; go straight to the Accident and Emergency ward of your local hospital; take the plant, berries or substance with you; try and find out how many tablets/berries/etc your child has swallowed.

6 Structural cloze

For questions 1–15, complete the following extract from a professional journal by writing each missing word in the space. Use only one word for each space. The exercise begins with an example.

Thinking about Family Life

Family life continues to occupy (0) *a* somewhat ambiguous position in public debate and policy in Britain today. On the one hand, references (1) .... the importance of the family, however defined (2) .... understood, (3) .... rarely absent from speeches at political party conferences or statements from religious leaders. On the (4) .... hand, (5) .... contrast to some other European countries, we do not have a minister (6) .... special responsibilities for 'the family' and (7) .... do we have anything (8) .... a coherent programme that could be called a family policy.

Some sociologists might lend their support to particular programmes or social policies, (9) .... the basis of the evidence as they see it. More (10) .... , however, the popular impression would seem to be (11) .... the sociologists provide the facts about family life and that (12) .... facts, thus 'discovered', provide the basis for public statements or, possibly, public policy. For (13) .... , sociologists may provide facts about the circumstances of lone mothers and (14) .... children and these studies (15) .... inform policy-makers.

7 Word formation

For questions 1–15, read the two texts below. Use the words in the boxes to form one word that fits in the same numbered space in the text. The exercise begins with an example (0).

Gender on Screen

Many (0) *researchers* have suggested that the media portray men and women in different and often (1) .... ways, arguing that this can lead to the (2) .... of gender stereotyping. (3) .... films are sometimes considered to be a 'male' genre with a limited range of characters for audience (4) .... Stallone, Schwarzenegger, Willis and Van Damme are (5) .... names, whose character types are fairly (6) .... .The subject (here) of such movies will usually be male, white, young, aggressive, vengeful, strong, invulnerable and (7) .... , using weapons and moving the narrative along. It is (8) .... the body of the masculine hero that provides the focus of the spectators' gaze and visual pleasure.

0	RESEARCH
1	LIMIT
2	PRODUCE
3	ACT
4	ENJOY
5	HOUSE
6	PREDICT
7	EMOTION
8	PRIMARY

Nappy Alarm

Some babies bawl when they have a wet nappy, others carry on gurgling (9) .... , leaving their mothers none the wiser and the baby at risk of nappy rash. Now novice British inventor, Paul Kimsey, has come up with a (10) .... alarm which warns parents when it's time to change their baby's wet nappy. The electronic device placed in the nappy alerts the parent by sounding a (11) .... bleeper carried on a belt or in a bag. Mr Kimsey, 36, came up with the idea seven years ago after witnessing the (12) .... suffered by a relative's baby. He was (13) .... to develop it at the time as he was too busy running the family car mat manufacturing business. He has fine-tuned his idea (14) .... since that first (15) ....

---

9 CONTENT
10 RELY
11 WARN
12 COMFORT
13 ABLE
14 CONSIDER
15 BRAIN

---

8 Wordcheck – Relationships

Complete the sentences below with vocabulary connected with relationships. The first letter of each word is given to help you. See the example.

1 Often the most difficult part of a relationship is asking the person out on the first date.
2 People looking for a partner sometimes place advertisements in the l...............-h............... column of a newspaper or magazine.
3 An a............... a............... is someone who gives advice to people who write to a magazine about their personal lives.
4 On their wedding day, the woman is the b............... and the man is the g............... .
5 After getting married most couples hold a r............... to which they invite all their friends and relatives.

6 The day after that, they usually go on their h............... – a romantic holiday for two!
7 A man with no intention of getting married may be described as a c............... b............... .
8 An o............... f............... is someone from your past who you used to have a romantic relationship with.
9 A w............... is a man whose wife has died.
10 On official forms you may be asked to state your m............... s............... , in other words whether you are married or not.
11 S............... is another word which often appears on official forms. It means husband or wife.
12 A famous male actor or singer adored by female fans is a h...............-............... .

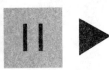

11 ▶ Last Chance to See

1 Relative clauses

▶ **Study Box, SB page 188**

1.1 Relative clauses – punctuation

Decide if the following sentences, which all contain relative clauses, are punctuated correctly or not. Make any necessary corrections, as in the example.

1 Mark's father **,** who used to be a diplomat **,** speaks eight foreign languages.
2 Children, who don't have brothers or sisters, often find it hard when they first go to school.
3 Have you still got that second-hand computer you bought from that chap you met in the pub we used to go to?
4 The Irish doctor, **who** used to work at this surgery, has moved to Leeds.
5 Do you remember that little cinema we saw all those old black and white movies at? Well, it's been pulled down!
6 We went to the first performance of the play which turned out to be a complete disaster!
7 It rained all day which meant we couldn't go out at all.
8 DNA which is 98.4% identical in humans and chimpanzees was discovered by Watson and Crick in 1944.
9 The Paris which is in Texas has very little to do with the Paris in France.
10 'Zorro', Mrs Nimmo's favourite cat whose tail was bitten off by a dog isn't very good at balancing any more!

1.2 Relative clauses with prepositions

Some of the relative clauses below are not acceptable either in terms of grammar or level of formality. Make any necessary corrections as in the example.

1 The person ~~that~~ you need to speak to is out of the office at present.
2 What was the name of that card game you were talking about?
3 The vegetation on that these animals depend is under threat.
4 Oh, look! There's that pen for which you've been looking.
5 We have established that this is the window through which the criminals made good their escape.
6 Although his parents called him Marcus, 'Ginger' was the name who he was generally known by.
7 But that chap from whom we bought the car said it was guaranteed!
8 The process the vast majority of nuclear power is produced by is known as 'fission'.
9 The department for which Mr Roberts is responsible has again failed to reach its production targets.
10 Those kids after whom she looks are really terrible!

2 Phrasal verbs

2.1 Tense and structure

Complete the following sentences with phrasal verbs from the box below. Use the correct tense or structure. An example is given.

carry out	cut down	cut up
dip into	hold up	make up
spring up		

1 Are all animals' bodies *made up* of cells?
2 Don't forget to .... the potatoes into small pieces before boiling them or they take ages.
3 It's not quite the sort of book you'd want to read from cover to cover but it's quite interesting to .... now and then.
4 It's a miracle the roof didn't fall in as one of the walls which had been .... it .... suddenly collapsed.

5 Modern computers are capable of ....
   .... the most complex operations in
   micro-seconds.
6 A lot of fast food restaurants have ....
   .... in the town centre over the last couple
   of years.
7 You need fifteen players to ....
   .... a rugby team.
8 We had to .... the old oak
   tree after it was damaged in the storm.

2.2 Different meanings

Use a good English/English dictionary to find different
uses for the phrasal verbs in the box in 2.1 and complete
the sentences, using the right tense. The first one is
shown as an example.

1 It took me over an hour to get *made up* for the part
   of Othello.
2 If you want to lose weight, you should ....
   .... on the amount of dairy products you
   eat.
3 He .... some story about
   catching the wrong train to explain his lateness.
4 Joe and Sally are always having quarrels but they
   always .... in the end.
5 The start of the concert ....
   by the late arrival of the group.
6 I can't afford a summer holiday this year unless I
   .... my savings.
7 Three masked men tried to ....
   .... the security van last week.
8 Monty accidentally trod on the rake, which
   .... and hit him on the
   nose!

3 Expressing the future

▶Focus on Grammar, SB page 189

**Put the verbs in brackets in the most suitable form
(active or passive) of the future. The first one has been
done for you.**

1 *Are you doing* (do) anything special on Friday
   evening?
2 Mandy .... (finish) her exams by this time
   next week.
3 The train .... (get) in at 5.15, which
   means we .... (have) about half an hour
   to get to the conference centre.
4 Look out! That boy .... (fall) of his bike!
5 The new sports centre .... (open) next
   month but I doubt if it .... (complete) by
   then!
6 The Prince .... (give) a speech to local
   community leaders this evening.
7 We .... (live) in this house for exactly five
   years next Sunday.
8 Congratulations! We hope you .... (be)
   very happy together.
9 The play .... (not start) until 8.30 so I think
   we .... (have) time to eat something first.
10 'Anna looks rather fat these days.'
    'Oh, don't you know? She .... (have) a baby.'
11 Just think, this time on Thursday we ....
    (fly) to Los Angeles.
12 Don't worry, I .... (phone) the plumber
    first thing tomorrow morning.
13 Do you think you .... (finish) that report
    by the end of the week?
14 .... I .... (give) you a lift to the
    airport on Monday or .... Fred
    .... (take) you?
15 We'd better hurry up, I think they ....
    (close).

4 Quantifiers – *each*/*every*, *either*/*neither*, etc

Focus on Grammar, SB page 192

Correct any incorrect uses of quantifiers in the following sentences. The first one is shown as an example.

1 None *of* the supermarkets in our town sells fresh fish.
2 Our two children are very alike: every one has red hair and green eyes.
3 Which of these two umbrellas is yours? None.
4 How much are these second-hand books? £1 every one.
5 You can go either way at the fork in the road: they all lead to the beach.
6 Is Phyllis a nurse or a dentist? Neither. She's a psychiatrist.
7 I'm afraid I know a few words of Italian so I can't really communicate.
8 All student is responsible for cleaning his own room.
9 Each CD in her collection was by the same group!
10 There seems a little point in continuing our discussion if you are not prepared to make any concessions.
11 We asked a young couple for directions but none of them knew where the street was.
12 I've seen all Meryl Streep's films and she's brilliant in every one.
13 We're having a cocktail party for few close friends next Friday if you'd like to join us.
14 Does either of them happen to live in Cavendish Road?
15 Each tyre on the car had been deliberately slashed by vandals.

STUDY TIP *both* and *all*

▶ These are placed after auxiliary verbs but before main verbs:
e.g. They can both/all swim.
Do you both/all speak French?
They have both/all been to New Zealand.
We both/all have black tea for breakfast.

---

5 Linking and logical devices – cause and result, purpose and time

Complete the following sentences with suitable linking devices. An asterisk (*) indicates at least two possible answers. Look at the example provided.

1 It was necessary to use a microscope *in order to/so as to/to* establish the existence of organisms in the drinking water.
2 They got to the shop at 6 a.m. * .... they would be able to get the best bargains in the sale.
3 You'd better take your cheque book with you .... it costs more than you expect.
4 The apple crop this year has been terrible * .... the unseasonal frosts we had in May.
5 * .... there was a train strike, we had to spend an extra two days on Otranto.
6 The man was .... rude .... the manager had to ask him to leave the restaurant.
7 Vince didn't get to bed until 5 a.m. .... he's feeling exhausted this morning.
8 Erica's new boss turned out to be .... a tyrant .... she resigned after a week!
9 The new model is slightly larger and * .... more expensive.
10 * .... you arrive in Bombay, give us a call to let us know everything's OK.
11 We won't be able to forward the goods * .... we receive your cheque.
12 .... I had the chance to reverse into the parking space someone else drove straight into it.
13 * .... had I dropped off to sleep .... next door's dog started howling at the moon.
14 .... he ate all the sandwiches. * .... he drank all the wine. .... he collapsed on the sofa!
15 .... Steve was upstairs having a shower, the burglars were downstairs helping themselves to his stereo, computer and TV.

6 Writing – Formal letter

The following letter is in response to the job advertisement shown below.
Complete the letter with suitable words or phrases. Look at the example.

DESK EDITOR

CIRCA £13,500 p.a.

An experienced editor is required by an expanding publisher of books on leisure, craft and wood-related subjects. The position involves taking charge of the day-to-day process of producing highly illustrated books from receipt of manuscript to approval for press. A practical approach is needed, with good keyboard and organisational skills, as well as the ability to work quickly and accurately to tight deadlines.

You will need to be able to work independently, although you will be part of a small team, and to be concerned with maintaining the highest standards.

Please apply in writing to:
Mr A E Phillips, Publisher
GMC Publications
166 High Street,
Lewes,
East Sussex BN7 1XU

```
                                          34 St Mary's Way
                                          Buxton
                                          Derbyshire BU4 8JS

                                          (1) 14th October 20–

Mr A E Phillips

GMC Publications
(2) . . . . . . . . . .
Lewes
East Sussex BN7 1XU

Dear Mr Phillips
I am interested (3) . . . . . . . . . . for the (4) . . . . . . . . . . desk editor
which (5) . . . . . . . . . . in 'The Independent' yesterday.
   (6) . . . . . . . . . . applying is that I (7) . . . . . . . . . . for 10 years as
an assistant editor in a small publishing company concerned mainly
with books on leisure and hobbies and I am now (8) . . . . . . . . . . a
post which would (9) . . . . . . . . . . more responsibility and independence
to make editorial and organisational decisions.
   I am used to and enjoy the challenge (10) . . . . . . . . . . to tight
deadlines to produce high quality books. I have fast and accurate
keyboard skills and am familiar with all modern publishing computer
software.
   I would be able (11) . . . . . . . . . . interview at any time which is
(12) . . . . . . . . . . to you.

(13) . . . . . . . . . .
(14) . . . . . . . . . .
```

Olivia James
(15) . . . .

7 Discourse cloze

For questions 1–5, read through the following article and then choose from the list A–J the best phrase given below it to fill each of the spaces. Some of the suggested answers do not fit at all. The exercise begins with an example (0).

Small is Beautiful

Fritz Schumacher, most famous for his work 'Small is beautiful', wasn't really an environmentalist at all. He was an economist, a philosopher, a wordsmith, a baker of bread and planter of trees and, together with Barbara Ward, one of the first pioneers (0) ..J. sustainable growth.

The subtitle of *Small is Beautiful* is 'Economics as if people mattered'. And that informs all his economic writing. It was, for instance, incomprehensible to Schumacher that politicians could so obsessively pursue the goal of endless economic growth (1) .... .

If idolised as the most essential task of society, economic growth bears bitter fruit and tends to defeat itself. Set it up as the supreme national objective and you will inevitably promote greed, impatience, ruthlessness and envy, destroying those fundamental virtues (2) .... .

But he was no believer in zero-growth either, (3) .... . 'To replace the idea of rapid economic growth by the idea of zero growth, that is to say, of organised stagnation, is to replace one emptiness with another.'

That kind of pragmatic balancing act is classic Schumacher doctrine (4) .... . It characterises his lifelong preoccupation with the scale of things; it wasn't that he thought everything big was automatically ugly but rather that we'd lost the art of gauging 'human scale' in terms of what works best in practice for individuals and society. .

In the gentlest of ways, he often remonstrated with environmentalists for being oblivious to such social and economic concerns. He couldn't understand why they were more concerned with the damage being done to wildlife than with that being done to the human mind (5) .... – 'the rotting of brains of millions of workers could be classed as the worst pollution of all.'

A even though this was the standard ecoposition in those days
B without which society cannot function satisfactorily
C and typical of environmentalists of his day
D through exposure to degrading and soulless work
E of the classic all-consuming capitalist Western civilisation
F without ever assessing the real benefits they derive from that growth
G and often advocated the benefits of 'a culture of poverty'
H and one of the reasons he is still so relevant
I without any form of quality of life
J of what we now call

8 Wordcheck – The environment

Match the two-word collocations in columns A and B and then use them to complete the sentences below. The first one is shown as an example.

A

illegal ~~water~~ rare forest
national long natural conservation
logging lead-free

B

petrol policy habitat lifespan
poaching species parks fire
~~shortage~~ rights

1 Climate change and desertification is leading to serious *water shortages* for people, animals and plants in some countries.

2 The use of .... is being promoted to improve air quality in many large cities with a great deal of traffic.

3 Every developing country needs a clear .... to avoid destroying their natural resources for quick money.

4 A large area of vegetation and many animals were destroyed in the ....

5 The White Rhino is now a very .... indeed with only a few thousand animals still alive.

6 .... for ivory accounts for the slaughter of hundreds of 'protected' adult elephants every year.

7 Larger mammals often have a very .... – some live for over 120 years!

8 Selling the .... to ancient forests results in only short-term wealth and long-term environmental disaster.

9 With so many forest areas being destroyed, a great deal of wildlife is losing its ....

10 Many countries now see the advantages of setting up .... in which animals and plants are legally protected.

Progress Test Three

Units 9 – 11

1 Structural cloze

For questions 1–15, complete the following passage by **writing each missing word in the space. Use one word only for each space. The exercise begins with an example (0).**

A mountain excursion

My friend, Nigel, (0) ....*who*........ had just completed an advanced orienteering course, had somehow (1) .... me to go on an excursion across the mountains with him. When we set out just after lunch, it had been clear and sunny but for the past hour or so it had been getting foggier and foggier. We had been walking along under a blanket of thick fog for about half an hour (2) .... Nigel suddenly turned to me and announced we were lost!

'Oh, that's marvellous!' I said. 'First of all you (3) .... me come on this stupid hike with you, you lead me up a mountain in the fog and now you tell me we're lost! I thought you knew (4) .... to read a map.'

'I (5) .... ,' protested Nigel. 'it's just that all the landmarks have been covered by this fog.'

'OK, OK, but it's getting dark now, what are we going to do?' I asked.
'We'll have to find somewhere to spend the night,' he said ominously.
We walked on a little way (6) .... we came up against an old stone wall (7) .... seemed to be part of an old farmhouse (8) .... I supposed had been abandoned by its former occupants.

'Well, it looks like survival tactics from now on,' said Nigel, apparently enjoying the idea. 'The (9) .... it gets, the better I like it,' he added with a grin, (10) .... me to wonder if he wasn't getting a little overexcited.

'Right, (11) .... we need now is some firewood. (12) .... I go and get some, you stay here and unpack the survival kit from the bottom of my rucksack,' ordered Nigel as he disappeared into the fog.

(13) .... about five minutes, he came back with an armful of sticks which appeared to have been cut into convenient lengths and just left on the mountain.

'OK, I'm going to try and fix up a shelter against the wall. In the (14) .... , you get a fire started,' he barked.

No (15) .... had I got the fire started than I heard a movement. I turned round to see a little old lady looking at me rather angrily.

'What on earth do you think you're doing in my field? For goodness sake put that wood back, I need it to repair the fence with.'

2 Phrasal verbs

Complete each of the following sentences with the appropriate form of a suitable phrasal verb. An example is provided.

Example: I enjoy *looking through* the encyclopaedia from time to time.

1 Sheila .... her duties well enough but she's just not interested in her job.
2 When I woke up, everyone else had gone to bed and the fire had ....
3 We were on holiday there when the civil war ....
4 Don't forget to .... your job application before this Friday.
5 There was so much snow that our village was completely .... and food had to be brought in by helicopter.

3 Error correction

In most of the lines of the following text there is a mistake connected with the verbs (tense, form, agreement, etc). <u>Underline</u> each mistake and write the correction in the space at the end of the line. If there is no mistake in a line, put a tick (✓) in the space. The exercise begins with two examples (0).

Solving the elk problem

Motorists who find themselves driving along the lonely roads
through Sweden's extensive pine forests <u>were</u> more relaxed these
days. Small plastic bottles which are being hung from roadside
trees had calmed their deepest fear – colliding with an elk!
  Each bottle contain a pungent blend of animal fat and wolf's
urine. The idea is simple – because wolves are hunting elks the
smell makes the elks to avoid the roads like the plague.
  'It really works, we're very exciting about it,' said spokesman
Lars Olofson, adding that 25,000 accidents have been caused
by elks every year, according to research he's just completed.
  The cost of protecting the roads will have been cut by the new
potion, which cost only 2 krona per metre compared with 40
krona per metre for the traditional metal fences used before.
  The wolf cocktail had been invented two years ago by Mr
Olofson's father, who used it to stop elks to eat his onions.
  'It's a top-secret formula,' added Lars, 'if everyone started
using it, the elks would soon have become desensitised to it
and perhaps they would no longer feared their old enemy – the wolf!'

0	✓
0	*are*
1	....
2	....
3	....
4	....
5	....
6	....
7	....
8	....
9	....
10	....
11	....
12	....
13	....
14	....
15	....
16	....

4 Discourse cloze

For questions 1–6, read through the following text and then choose from the list A–J the best phrase to fit each of the spaces. Write one letter (A–J) in the spaces. The exercise begins with an example (0).

Mystery of the dying frogs

Many of the world's amphibians, particularly frogs and toads, are becoming extinct faster than scientists can determine the causes. At the Third World Congress of Herpetology, held in Prague in August, (0) ..J.. . Serious declines and several probable extinctions have been reported from the Pacific North West of America, from Central America and from Western Australia. While most amphibian declines around the world are attributable to habitat destruction (1) .... , some species (but not all) have declined rapidly in nature reserves, national parks and other areas (2) .... .

Karen Lips, of the Smithsonian Tropical Research Institute in Panama, has found large numbers of dead and dying frogs along streams. The disease which has killed them seems to be moving southwards through the mountains of Central America. One symptom is a thickening of the skin, (3) .... . This appears to be caused by a protozoan parasite. A similar organism may also be responsible for the deaths of thousands of frogs in the mountains of Queensland, Australia. Urgent research is under way (4) .... .

Typically, herpetologists have had to respond to these declines (5) .... . Now, recent work by Ross Alford, of James Cook University, Australia, has suggested one way to detect a decline early on; measure a frog's limbs. His study has shown that fluctuating asymmetry (random variation in the size of paired structures on the left and right side of the body) increases in the limbs of frogs (6) .... .

A to determine if this is indeed the case
B set aside for the protection of biodiversity
C as quickly as possible under the circumstances
D as their population size declines
E in all these three areas
F into the effects of DDT on amphibians in the US and Kenya
G after they have occurred
H which effectively smothers the frog
I which have built up immunity to such diseases
J it became clear that the phenomenon is a global one

5 Word formation

Read the texts below. Use the words in the boxes to form one word that fits in the same numbered spaces in the texts. The exercise begins with an example (0).

Afraid of giving

Just as women are afraid of receiving, so men are afraid of giving. To extend himself in giving to others means to risk (0) ......*failure*...... , correction and disapproval. These consequences are most (1) .... because deep inside his unconscious he holds an (2) .... belief that he is not good enough. This belief was formed and reinforced in (3) .... every time he thought he was expected to do better. When his (4) .... went unnoticed or were (5) .... , deep in his unconscious he began forming the belief that he was not good enough. A man is particularly vulnerable to this belief. It generates within him the fear of failing. He wants to give but is afraid he will fail, so he doesn't try. If his biggest fear is (6) .... , he is naturally going to avoid any (7) .... risks.

Cross-cultural misunderstandings

Many visitors to Britain find the natives' (8) .... frequently rather strange and occasionally totally (9) .... One of the most common complaints is that we are cold and (10) .... In fact, all we are trying to do is to 'mind our own business' and not to interfere in other people's. This may also make us appear (11) .... in foreign visitors. We are also seen as far too (12) .... , forever going round saying 'Sorry' and 'I beg your pardon'. Again, our main concern is to avoid any degree of (13) .... On the other hand, foreign visitors often appear (unintentionally) (14) .... to the British. What to a Spaniard is a wholly (15) .... click of the fingers to attract attention is highly insulting to a British barworker and practically guarantees a drink-free evening!

0	FAIL
1	PAIN
2	CORRECT
3	CHILD
4	ACCOMPLISH
5	APPRECIATE
6	ADEQUATE
7	NECESSARY

8	BEHAVE
9	COMPREHEND
10	FRIEND
11	INTEREST
12	APOLOGY
13	EMBARRASS
14	POLITE
15	OFFEND

Living Dangerously

1 Collocations and idioms

Fill in the gaps in the sentences below to create suitable collocations and idioms connected with risk and danger. The first one has been done for you.

1 Chris was cautioned by the police for *exceeding* the speed limit.
2 Every time you make a parachute jump you're taking your life in your own h....................... .
3 Modern society has become so 'safe' that people pay good money to e....................... themselves to more risk!
4 Teenagers often show a r....................... disregard for their own safety.
5 Val was d....................... with death, driving so fast on an icy road.
6 The popularity of so-called a....................... holidays is indicative of how important thrills are in our lives.
7 This crossroads is a notorious accident b....................... – five people have been killed here in the last six months.
8 People need to be trained to deal with fires before they get out of h....................... .
9 An enormous crowd gathered to watch the motorbike riders do their d....................... stunts.
10 We had a really n....................... escape – the avalanche missed our cabin by a few metres.
11 You're really playing with f....................... if you agree to take part in that dishonest deal.
12 I'm not risking my n....................... in that old car. I'd rather walk!
13 With no money and nowhere to spend the night, Walter was in a bit of a tight c....................... .
14 George is skating on very thin i....................... – one more mistake and the boss is going to fire him.
15 Going into my headmaster's study really felt like entering the lion's d....................... – I was terrified!

2 Emphatic structures

Rewrite the following sentences to make them more emphatic. Look at the underlined words and any other words given in brackets to help you. See the example in number one.

1 We'd never seen such a huge wolf.
   Never had we seen such a huge wolf.
2 I'd really like to try bungee-jumping. (The thing …)
3 The greatest cause of accidents is inexperience not recklessness.
4 There wasn't a fire escape anywhere in the entire hotel!
5 Visitors must not approach the cages under any circumstances.
6 Most young people need a sense of danger in their lives. (What …)
7 We didn't see a living soul for over two months!
8 They weren't rescued until three days after the accident. (It …)
9 She'd no sooner left hospital than she went sky-diving again!
10 I really love the rush of adrenalin I get when I go skiing.

3 Phrasal verbs

▶Language check, SB page 205

3.1 Tense and structure

Complete the following sentences with phrasal verbs from the box below. Use the right tense or structure. The first one is shown as an example.

| ~~break out~~ | bring out | cut off |
| get over | put down to | put out |

1 Quick action by the police prevented fighting from *breaking out* between rival groups of fans after the football match.
2 Sports commentators have .... her poor performance .... lack of training.
3 The magazine article .... the more unpleasant side to the actor's personality.
4 The gas supply was .... for about four hours as they had to repair some leaking pipes.

5 Herbie asked them to .... their cigarettes as he is allergic to smoke.

6 As Consuelo didn't speak any English, it was rather difficult for her to .... what she wanted us to do.

7 In the Middle Ages, there was very little you could do if a smallpox epidemic .... near your home.

8 I phoned to let them know which plane I'd be on but I was .... before I could tell them.

3.2 Different meanings

Use a good English/English dictionary to find different uses for the phrasal verbs in the box in 3.1. The first one has been done for you.

1 I hear FIAT have *brought out* a new model but I haven't seen it yet.

2 I know they split up over three years ago but he's never really .... her.

3 Jack shouldn't have spent so much time and money on the publicity campaign – still, he'll just have to .... it .... experience.

4 He looked a bit different last time I saw him, maybe because he'd .... his ponytail ....

5 She .... the problem of lack of time by hiring a house-cleaner.

6 The prison is supposed to be high security but twelve prisoners .... last month.

7 The radio station .... a warning about the severe weather only minutes before it arrived!

8 She's an exceptional teacher. She .... the best in all her pupils.

4 Past tenses

▶Focus on Grammar, SB page 205

Correct any mistakes you find in the following sentences. Not all of them are wrong. See the example given.

1 There was a power cut while we ~~watched~~ *were watching* the film on TV last night.

2 Did you ever get into trouble at school when you were a kid?

3 Florencia never saw snow until she went to Scotland.

4 Just how many patients did Dr Harris examine so far this week?

5 Oh, what a lovely hat! Where have you bought it?

6 Mr Wolf has worked at the bank for 25 years before his retirement last May.

7 I've been writing ten letters this morning – I need a rest!

8 By the time we got to the theatre the play already started.

9 How long did you live in Italy for? Three years but then I got homesick.

10 I was sitting on the train for ten minutes when I realised I'd left my suitcase on the platform!

11 Exactly what were you doing at eleven o'clock yesterday evening, sir?

12 When I looked out of the window, I realised it had snowed for hours and there was no chance of getting back down the mountain.

13 That's the third time Sam crashed the car this month!

14 Just think, this time last week we rode a camel in the desert!

15 Of course it has rained. Look how wet the road is.

5 Conditionals

▶ **Focus on Grammar, SB page 205**

5.1 Conditional 3

In the following sentences, put the verbs in brackets in the correct tense to form 3rd or mixed conditionals. Put any other words in brackets in the correct place. An example is given.

1 If I *hadn't seen* (not see) it with my own eyes, I *wouldn't have believed* (not believe) it!
2 We .... (still live) in Cardiff if we .... (not find) someone to buy our house last year.
3 If Hilary .... (look) out of the window at that moment, she .... (not spot) the criminals trying to break into her car.
4 Nobody .... (ever guess) he was a thief if he .... (not catch) red-handed taking money from the safe.
5 Henry .... (not ever get) that job at the bank if he .... (not go) to school with the manager's son.
6 Just think, if I .... (take) that job with the export/import company, I .... (live) in São Paulo now, not Manchester!
7 If the doctor .... (not notice) the defect when I was a child, I .... (be) practically blind by now.
8 We .... (be) home in bed ages ago if you .... (not lose) the map!
9 Frank .... (not be) here today if that boy .... (not know) how to do artificial respiration.
10 If you .... (listen) to the traffic report on the radio this morning, we .... (not sit) here in this jam!

5.2 1st, 2nd, 3rd and mixed conditionals

Rewrite the following sentences as conditionals. The first one is shown as an example.

1 Eric was with us so we didn't get lost.
  If *Eric hadn't been with us, we would have got lost.*
2 We got soaking wet on Sunday and now we've all got colds.
  If ....
3 I'm afraid I don't know so I can't tell you.
  If ....
4 Because the train was 10 minutes late I managed to catch it.
  I ....
5 The weather could be bad on Saturday, in which case we'll have to cancel the barbecue.
  We ....
6 I'm living in Italy because I got married to an Italian.
  I ....
7 Sorry I didn't phone you but I lost the bit of paper with your number on it.
  I ....
8 We don't get on very well because she's so aggressive.
  If ....
9 There's the possibility of a train strike on Monday so I might not be able to come.
  If ....
10 We've got a broken window because you and your friends were playing football in the back yard!
  We ....
11 They're so reserved that I speak to them very infrequently.
  I ....
12 I missed the end of the film so I don't know who the murderer was.
  If ....
13 Jimmie's father might buy him a new bike; it depends on him passing his exams.
  If ....
14 As we'd already seen the film we didn't go to the cinema.
  We ....
15 Zoe tripped and fell just as she was about to win the race.
  Zoe ....

STUDY TIP — Conditionals

▶ Each conditional has a more formal equivalent:

Type 1: If you arrive late, go straight to my office.
Should you arrive late, go straight to my office.

Type 2: If we reduced the price, we'd make no profit.
Were we to reduce the price, we'd make no profit.
(N.B. This is a very uncommon form.)

Type 3: If she had phoned, I would have met her.
Had she phoned, I would have met her.

6 Dependent prepositions

Complete the following sentences with the correct prepositions. The first one has been done as an example.

1 Exercising without first warming up can lead *to* injury.
2 John takes a very irresponsible attitude .... his own safety – he never wears a crash helmet.
3 We sat there speculating .... how the accident might have happened.
4 There were so many people queuing .... a go on the 'Wall of Death' that we decided to try the 'Ghost Train'.
5 Fiona's twisted ankle prevented her .... going skating.
6 Many people seem to enjoy exposing themselves .... risk.
7 You need to be able to devote a lot of time .... practice if you want to become a top athlete.
8 Walking in the snow for over six hours led .... frostbite in Carl's toes.
9 We spent loads of money .... new equipment for our camping holiday.
10 At weekends, our husbands indulge .... war games. They're like big kids really.

7 Writing – Article

You have been asked to write an article of about 250 words for a local newspaper advertising a new Adventure Park which is opening next week just outside the town. Expand the following notes to write your article to attract as many people as possible to the Park.

Name: Tamford Towers Adventure Park

Opening: next Saturday at noon

Cost: cheapest in Britain – lots of 'family deals'

Clients: suitable for all the family – toddlers, teenagers and adults, something for everybody

Rides: ten fantastic rides – full of thrills – ranging from traditional water splash (bit boring?) to 'Screwball'-type of crazy high-speed spinner and 'The Abyss' – vertical drop for 10 metres totally exhilarating and many others.

Other attractions: small zoo – penguins (feeding times 11 am and 5 pm), camels, rhinos and 'Uncle Ted's Farmyard' with chickens, sheep, goats, etc for younger kids

Facilities: large playground for little kids, cafe-style restaurant, pub, souvenir shop (full of great stuff), refreshment kiosks around the park, plenty of toilets, huge free car parking area!

8 Structural cloze

For questions 1–15, complete the following extract by writing each missing word in the space. Use only one word for each space. The exercise begins with an example.

A rescue (0) *was* underway in the Scottish Highlands last night (1) .... a team of six climbers fell 500ft on Creag Meagaidh in Inverness-shire. Initial reports (2) .... that several of the party were seriously injured. Helicopters from RAF Kinloss and HMS Gannet were scrambled (3) .... the scene of the accident, (4) .... happened around 4.30 pm yesterday. The RAF Sea King was flying the injured mountaineers to a rendezvous point from (5) .... the naval helicopter was taking (6) .... on to Raigmore Hospital, 35 miles (7) .... the north. A hospital spokesman said that (8) .... the six climbers, two were stretcher cases and the (9) .... four were 'walking wounded'.

It is understood the six climbers were all roped (10) .... when they came off the 3,700ft mountain, which (11) .... four miles north of the southern tip of Loch Laggan. The fall was witnessed by (12) .... team of climbers, (13) .... managed to raise the alarm shortly before 5 pm.

The Cairngorm and Lochaber mountain rescue teams, (14) .... with sister units from RAF Kinloss and Leuchars, were called (15) .... in the biggest night-time rescue operation in the Highlands this year.

9 Wordcheck – Fire

There are 18 words connected with fire and fire fighting in the box below. You will find 6 horizontally, 8 vertically and 4 diagonally. Three have been found for you.

```
C R T A S P A R K S T U R
F O E Y M D E M B E R S E
U R N B O I X A R L B O S
H A G F U B T P I N A T C
O V I L L R I F G E L Z U
S I N E D A N T A N A G E
E B E D E F G L D N R O F
K S P V R A U R E T M B I
A M C F M H I O A X C E R
E F L A M E S O M T L S E
W I G U P N H E A T I R M
I S M O K E E K T O L O A
H U T Y S A R S O N T A N
```

1 Pronouns – object, reflexive and reciprocal

Correct any mistakes in the use of pronouns in the following sentences. See the example in number one.

1 When her sister left home, Mary finally had a bedroom all to ~~her~~ *herself.*
2 OK. Let's meet ourselves outside the disco at ten.
3 Did you do all this by you or did someone help you?
4 We were shown around the factory by the Chairman himself.
5 Some of the people hurt itself trying to climb over the fence.
6 You should enclose a self-addressed envelope if you want them to send the material back to yourself.
7 John really prides himself on his Italian pronunciation and no one has the heart to tell him it's terrible!
8 I don't really understand it myself but my wife does.
9 How many other people from Bath went to the meeting besides you?
10 Oh come on, can't you make ourselves a cup of tea? I haven't got time.
11 I'm not surprised they're splitting up, they never really talked to themselves.
12 People say that talking to yourself is the first sign of madness.
13 Us as parents can fully understand how you must have felt.
14 We are looking for a penfriend for each of ourselves.
15 They arrived early in the morning and had the whole beach to them.
16 Nicola and Kim are so happy together, it's as though they were made for themselves.

2 Past tenses for hypothetical situations

▶ **Focus on Grammar, SB page 213**

Complete the sentences to express your thoughts for each of the following situations. Look at the example given.

1 Your dream is to be able to surf.
   I wish I could surf!

2 Your colleague keeps interrupting you when you're speaking.
   I'd rather you ....
3 It's ten to nine and your sister has to be at the station by nine!
   Come on, it's time you ....
4 You lost your temper at work this morning and now you're sorry.
   I wish I ....
5 Your brother is pretending not to have seen his old girlfriend.
   Why are you acting as though ....
6 You think your friend might lose his job and he should think about this possibility.
   But suppose you ....
7 A friend has rather stupidly given your phone number to an insurance agent.
   I'd rather you ....
8 Someone who's rather wealthy is always complaining about having no money.
   Oh, stop talking as if you ....
9 You're depressed because you have to go back to work tomorrow.
   If only I ....
10 A passenger on a boat stopped you from falling overboard by holding on to your belt!
   If he ....
11 The cold, cloudy British weather is getting you down.
   I really wish ....
12 You dream of being rich and travelling round the world in your own plane.
   If I ....

> **STUDY TIP** | Past tenses for hypothetical situations
>
> ▶ Remember that in English we use past tenses to talk about an imaginary action or state which isn't true/isn't happening or wasn't true/didn't happen:
> e.g. I wish she was happy. = she's not happy at the moment
> If only she'd studied for the exam. = she didn't study

3 Vocabulary

3.1 Word building ▶ Language Check, SB page 217

Complete the sentences below with suitable nouns or adjectives formed from the words given in brackets. See the example provided.

1 Tony is a terribly *competitive* (compete) person.
2 Most adolescents go through periods of great .... (insecure).
3 Limited exposure to the sun's rays can be .... (benefit) to health.
4 Daniel shows very little .... (aware) of how others see him.
5 The confusion over the diplomats' names caused a great deal of .... (embarrass).
6 Although she appeared calm, you could hear the .... (anxious) in her voice.
7 I've always regarded him as a man of great .... (sincere).
8 Monica was always very .... (resent) of the fact that she was never given the chance of going to university.
9 I'm really fed up with her air of superiority – she's just so .... (dismiss) of everyone else's ideas.
10 Oh, it's a delightful little restaurant. Tasteful decor, excellent food and, most important, ... (attend) waiters!

3.2 Adjectives

Make any necessary corrections to the adjectives in the sentences below. The mistake may be either of logic or word formation. The exercise starts with an example.

11 The British are generally regarded as an ~~inemotional~~ *unemotional* race.
12 What's wrong? You seem very uncontented with your job these days.
13 No one is completely unvulnerable to stress.
14 The police were not fooled by their unconvincing story.
15 I wouldn't trust him at all. He's one of the most unhonest men I know.
16 They seemed unaware that there was anyone else in the room.
17 The children were impatient for the film to start.
18 I couldn't help thinking that all their lavish praise was really unsincere.
19 I'm afraid Joan is very disattentive in lessons.
20 He's not very good-looking but, there again, he's not inattractive either.

4 Phrasal verbs

Fill in the gaps in the following passage with suitable phrasal verbs in the correct form. The first one has been done for you.

Top dogs and underdogs

The people I work with (1) *fall into* two main groups – those who do the bullying (the aggressors) and those who get bullied (the victims). Their distinctive behaviour is most apparent in meetings. The first thing that (2) .... them .... is their body language. I've even seen a 'victim' (3) .... their chair for an 'aggressor' and (4) .... standing for an hour instead! When it comes to speaking, a typical 'victim' will (5) .... in mid-sentence if an 'aggressor' so much as looks in their direction! And even when a 'victim' is talking heatedly about something important, an 'aggressor' can easily (6) .... him or her .... and state their own view. Not only that but after the meeting the 'victim' usually finds himself (7) .... the wishes of an 'aggressor'. Bearing all this in mind, I have decided to (8) .... all sorts of aspects of psychology and get each group to (9) .... the fact that they need to change their behaviour patterns.

5 Dictionary skills

In all of the following exercises you should use a good English/English dictionary to help you find the answers.

5.1 Collocations

Some of the following sentences, which contain actions and parts of the body you do them with, are incorrect. Correct any mistakes, as in the example.

fingers
1   Please stop drumming your ~~thumbs~~ on the table – it's driving me mad!
2   Steve screwed his face up in pain when he accidentally banged his head on the low doorway.
3   The station guard shrugged his arms unhelpfully when I asked him where the nearest bank was.
4   I couldn't help clapping my palms with joy when I heard I'd finally passed my driving test.
5   Bill's such a spoilt child – if he doesn't get his own way he stamps his legs and screams until you give in.
6   The old woman shook her fist at the children stealing apples from her garden.
7   Everyone nodded their necks in agreement at the director's proposal for increasing sales.
8   I cupped my hands and drank greedily from the mountain stream.

5.2 Metaphors and idioms

Match up the beginnings and endings of the following sentences and add a word from the box below to make a suitable metaphor or idiom.

ears	teeth	foot	nail	eye
teeth	heart	heels	thumbs	hand

9   Sally's prepared to fight tooth and .... ☐
10 I really put my .... in it ☐
11 When I was at school ☐
12 The debate got completely out of .... ☐
13 The train was about to leave as we got to the station ☐
14 It's no good warning Judy about Harry; ☐
15 I keep dropping things today; ☐
16 Robin lied through his .... ☐
17 Can you keep an .... on my luggage, ☐
18 Sorry, but I just can't make it to the dinner party; ☐

A   but we just caught it by the skin of our ....
B   to keep possession of her house.
C   when the police asked him about his movements last Friday evening.
D   I tried to learn Shakespeare's sonnets by ....
E   she's head over .... in love with him.
F   I'm up to my .... in work.
G   I've got to go to the toilet for a minute.
H   I seem to be all fingers and ....
I   when I asked her about her job – she's been sacked!
J   when two old ladies started hitting each other with their handbags.

STUDY TIP   Learning idioms and metaphors

▶ A good way to remember an idiom or a metaphor is to draw a picture of it (it doesn't have to be very good) – this will help you remember better than simply writing it down! Use the 4-column method shown below.

PICTURE	FIRST LETTERS	IDIOM	EXAMPLE SENTENCE
	k..... a..... e..... o.....	keep an eye on	Could you keep an eye on my bag while I go to the toilet
	o..... t..... b.....	have something on the brain	Robert must have golf on the brain – he never stops talking about it!

Once you have created this grid, you can test yourself by covering everything except the pictures with a piece of paper to see if you can remember. If you can't, slide the piece of paper to the right to reveal the first letter. Try it, it works.

6 Expressions of concession

▶ **Study box, SB page 218**

Use a suitable expression of concession to complete the following sentences. Initial letters are provided to help you. See the example.

1 *Although* she didn't have the right qualifications, she was offered the job.
2 We can't seem to save any money n................. m................. how hard we try!
3 M................. a................. we enjoyed our time in India, we wouldn't want to go and live there again.
4 They managed to find their way out of the jungle i................. s................. o................. not having a map or compass.
5 W................. we appreciate how much work you've put into the project, it's just not what we wanted.
6 You'll end up spending lots of money w................. airline you fly with.
7 H................. difficult it might seem now, you'll be glad you did it in the end.
8 D................. t................. f................. t................. they phoned well in advance, all the tickets had been sold.
9 I'm sorry but we're going to have to economise, w................. you might think.
10 H................. h................. we tried, we just couldn't make ourselves understood.

7 Vocabulary

▶ **Focus on Vocabulary, SB page 220**

Complete the following sentences with suitable **collocations connected with the body**. Initial letters are provided to help you. **The first one has been done for you.**

1 Jake sounded relaxed but his *body language* showed he was feeling threatened.
2 It was a h................. c................., so they were lucky nobody was killed.
3 We were so far away we tried to communicate using h................. s................. .
4 Steve wants a serious h................. t................. about our relationship - I'm dreading it!
5 I'm sorry. I spoke without thinking. It was a k................. r................. .
6 Annie gave us a quick .... s................. of her life as a double agent during the Cold War.
7 And then there was an e................. n................. as the gigantic wave crashed down on to the boat.
8 Carla is very insecure. She never makes e................. c................. when talking to you.
9 I have terrible b................. c................. . My toes turn blue in the winter months!
10 Judy told us a h................. s................. about finding giant spiders under the bed when she was living in the Amazon.

8 Word formation

For questions 1–15, read the two texts below. Use the words given to form one word that fits in the same numbered space in the text. The exercise begins with an example (0).

Take care in the sun

The sun should be enjoyed but (0) *overexposure* can cause sunburn, leading to (1) .... skin ageing and increased risk of skin cancer. It is the ultraviolet rays which cause this; even in the UK they can damage your skin, and UV is much more (2) .... the nearer the equator you go. You should stay out of the sun during the 2 hours around midday, use shade at other times, a sun hat and (3) .... woven but loose clothing. (4) .... creams suitable for your skin type can help protect (5) .... exposed parts of the body. A further sun related risk is heatstroke, caused by (6) .... Avoid strenuous activity during the hottest hours and make sure you drink plenty of (7) .... drinks (best is water which has been boiled or soft drinks from sealed cans or bottles) to replace body fluids.

Plastic surgery

Most impressive is Dr Ohana's (8) .... to the individual needs of his patients, honed by (9) .... experience and his earlier career as a doctor. Born in Marrakech in 1951, Ohana grew up in an (10) .... household. When Ohana was 10, however, his father severed the nerves and tendons of a hand and he could no longer play a musical instrument. Moved by the devastating effect this had on his father and his (11) .... route to (12) .... , Ohana decided to become a doctor. He became a surgeon, specialising in cancer patients. It was during this period that he learnt the (13) .... of finding out how patients feel (14) .... He believes it to be a crucial element in cosmetic surgery. 'No matter how able a surgeon is, the success of an operation depends entirely on why the patient has come for a (15) .... ,' he says.

0	EXPOSE
1	MATURE
2	POWER
3	TIGHT
4	PROTECT
5	AVOID
6	HEAT
7	ALCOHOL

8	SENSITIVE
9	CHILD
10	ART
11	PAIN
12	RECOVER
13	IMPORTANT
14	EMOTION
15	CONSULT

8 Writing – Character reference

Read through the following character reference written for someone who has applied for a job as a member of staff at an exclusive Health Farm and make any changes you think are necessary. See the example.

~~About my acquaintance~~ Ms Maria Hempel

Dear Sir or Madam,

I'm dropping you a line in support of Ms Maria Hempel's application to become a resident health and fitness trainer at your place. I've known Maria for getting on for about ten years in her job as aerobics instructor at the gym which I'm manager of – 'Avalon Club' is its name.

The first thing I must say about her is that she's brilliant at teaching aerobics. The feedback forms I get people to fill in have all rated her extremely highly. The only little niggle some of the older people had was with her pink hair but I expect she'll change that if she gets the job at your posh place.

I also know she has been following a health and nutrition course and has just passed the exams and got another certificate.

But Maria is not just a good instructor she's also always on time, never away through illness, and a humorous and well-liked member of the gym instructors' team who gets on like a house on fire with everybody.

In a nutshell, I'd say Maria will make an excellent member of staff for you. We'll all be sad to see her go from here and I'll certainly find it hard to get anyone as good as her again.

Best wishes,

Jim Long

14 ▶ Testing Times

1 Review of grammatical and syntactical structures

▶ **Focus on Grammar, SB page 229**

Most (but not all) of the sentences in the following sections contain classic mistakes. Correct those you find. See the example provided.

1.1 Tense forms and time

1 By this time next month we ~~will finish~~ all our exams! *will have finished*
2 I'd rather you don't smoke indoors. Can't you go out on the balcony?
3 Is this the first time you taste Spanish food?
4 You're always leaving the lights on – it's a terrible waste of energy!
5 I really wish I was born somewhere warm, like Australia!

1.2 Conditionals

1 If only you told me it was her birthday, I'd have brought a present.
2 If you'll offer us a larger discount, we'll pay within ten working days.
3 To be honest, we'll all be quite relieved unless he comes to the meeting.
4 We'd be back in the tent now if you didn't lose the map.
5 Had we not seen the rock in time, we would definitely have crashed.

1.3 Structures after verbs

1 They tried to stop us to play cricket in the park.
2 She suggested me to speak to the Principal about my problem.
3 I'm interested to learn as much about Zimbabwe as possible before my trip next month.
4 Remember buying a card for your mother. It's her birthday next week.
5 The printer seems to be broken. Why don't you try to plug it in?

1.4 Modals/Modal perfects

1 Don't touch that – I think it can be poisonous!

2 It mustn't have been Jack you spoke to, he doesn't work here any more.
3 Although he had broken his leg, he could swim to the shore.
4 Might you have left your handbag on the bus, do you think?
5 They told us we needn't have taken warm clothes but when we got there it was absolutely freezing.

1.5 Passives

1 By the time we got to the canteen, most of the food was already eaten.
2 Having been made redundant, Josh decided to emigrate.
3 I think my eyes need being tested, I keep getting terrible headaches.
4 Members are requested to provide proof of identity.
5 Unfortunately, Rory's record collection got damaged when he moved house.

1.6 Linking devices

1 Despite he lived in Germany for a year, he couldn't speak a word of the language.
2 We had to cancel the course due of the low number of enrolments.
3 The reason for she studied languages was to work as a tour guide.
4 Poor dietary habits are a major reason of heart disease.
5 Football is an exciting spectator sport, however cricket can be rather boring.

1.7 Participle clauses

1 Lived in the countryside as a boy, I missed out on a lot of things.
2 Suddenly I recognised the man lying in the shop doorway.
3 Never flying before, Ronald seemed rather anxious just before take-off.
4 Terry learnt to ski while living in Canada.
5 My mother who lives in Bath is a school teacher.

1.8 Emphatic structures

1 No sooner we'd arrived at the bar when it closed.
2 Not only dirty was the hotel room, it was also freezing cold!

3 Only when the detective turned over the body did he realise the full horror of the crime.

4 What do we want is a direct answer not yet another carefully prepared speech.

5 That's not right. It was Tchaikovsky who wrote the '1812 Overture' not Mozart.

2 -ing forms

2.1 ... -ing or infinitive?

Match up the beginnings and endings of the following sentences and add a suitable verb either with -ing or in the infinitive. Look at the example.

1 The train had to stop suddenly   E
2 I'd been calling our dog for ages
3 Poor Alison absolutely dreads ....
4 I remember .... it in a safe place
5 I meant .... you a ring to tell you I'd be late
6 Polly tried .... happy and relaxed
7 British Rail regrets .... passengers
8 Why don't you try .... the car –
9 The doctor forgot .... me how often
10 After a few weeks working with Gwendoline
11 Will you remember .... the gas bill
12 I dread .... what would have happened
13 Victor really regrets .... university
14 I'll never forget .... mistaken

A I had to take the tablets.
B or had I better do it myself?
C but everyone could see she'd been crying.
D but I just didn't have the time.
E *to avoid* crashing into a cow standing on the tracks!
F for a famous actor when I arrived at Madrid airport.
G if the lifeguard hadn't seen you.
H that all trains are subject to delay due to the snow.
I I came .... what an extraordinary person she was.
J before he came .... out of the wood with a rabbit in his mouth.
K but I've no idea where!
L before completing his degree.
M that might get it started?
N and has to take half a bottle of tranquillisers before she'll set foot on a plane.

2.2 -ing forms, infinitive with or without to

In the following sentences, circle the correct form of the verbs in bold. The first one is shown as an example.

1 I'd rather not **to/go/going** very far in the new car until I've got used **to/drive/driving** it.
2 Max dreads **to/be/being** made redundant as he's too old **to/get/getting** another decent job.
3 I spent all afternoon **to/listen/listening** to the neighbours **to/argue/arguing** about whose turn it was to mow the lawn.
4 I noticed the girl **to/put/putting** the watch into her pocket without **to/pay/paying** for it.
5 Hadn't you better **to/start/starting to/revise/revising** for the exam?
6 I think Rodney rather resents Jessica **to/participate/participating** in the conference.
7 The fire brigade had **to/be/being** called **to/get/getting** the boys down from the roof.
8 Why not **to/go/going** by train rather than **to/take/taking** the car?
9 Louise always hated her father **to/tell/telling** her what to do.
10 The council was **to/ban/banning** all parking in the city centre but there were so many complaints they've decided not to.
11 I didn't dare **to/show/showing** them the damage I'd done to their car.
12 We're bound **to/run/running** out of cash so don't forget **to/bring/bringing** your credit card.
13 If this is a private matter, perhaps you'd prefer me **to/leave/leaving**.
14 Our physical education teacher used **to/make/making** us **to/go/going** swimming in an outdoor pool even in winter.

STUDY TIP -ing or infinitive

▶ With the verbs *remember, forget, regret* and *stop* the choice between -*ing* or the infinitive depends on whether the verb following them happens before or after.
-*ing* = before
infinitive = after
e.g. Do you remember *meeting* me last year?
meeting happened before *remember*
Did you remember *to post* that letter?
to post happened (or not) after *remember*

3 Tenses

Decide which tense is being described in each 'time line' and short description and then write an example sentence in that tense. A cross shows an individual action or event and a wavy line shows an activity happening continuously or repeatedly. Look at the example given.

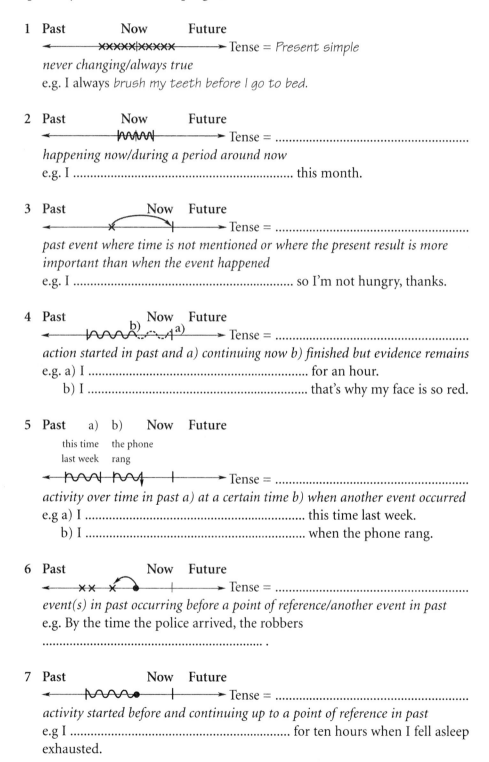

1   Past   Now   Future

    ← ✗✗✗✗✗|✗✗✗✗✗ → Tense = *Present simple*

    never changing/always true

    e.g. I always *brush my teeth before I go to bed.*

2   Past   Now   Future

    ← ∿∿∿ → Tense = ...

    happening now/during a period around now

    e.g. I .... this month.

3   Past   Now   Future

    ← ✗⌒| → Tense = ...

    past event where time is not mentioned or where the present result is more important than when the event happened

    e.g. I .... so I'm not hungry, thanks.

4   Past   Now   Future

    ← ∿∿∿∿....⌐ᵃ⁾ → Tense = ...

    action started in past and a) continuing now b) finished but evidence remains

    e.g. a) I .... for an hour.

        b) I .... that's why my face is so red.

5   Past   a) b)   Now   Future

          this time   the phone
          last week   rang

    ← ∿∿∿ ∿∿| | → Tense = ...

    activity over time in past a) at a certain time b) when another event occurred

    e.g a) I .... this time last week.

        b) I .... when the phone rang.

6   Past   Now   Future

    ← ✗✗ ✗⌒● | → Tense = ...

    event(s) in past occurring before a point of reference/another event in past

    e.g. By the time the police arrived, the robbers

    ....

7   Past   Now   Future

    ← ∿∿∿● | → Tense = ...

    activity started before and continuing up to a point of reference in past

    e.g I .... for ten hours when I fell asleep exhausted.

8 Past   Now   Future

←———┼——〰●〰—→ Tense = ...

activity seen as occurring around a stated time/reference point in the future
e.g. I .... this time next month.

9 Past   Now   Future

←———┼——××—●——→ Tense = ...

future event(s) happening before another future event/point of reference
e.g I hope I .... when I meet her next week.

10 Past   Now   Future

←〰〰〰〰〰●——→Tense = ...

activity started before and continuing up to a future point of reference
e.g. I .... for three years next June.

4 Review of tenses

In the following passage, put the verbs in brackets into a suitable (active or passive) tense and put any adverbial expressions in the correct place. The first one has been done for you.

I must admit that Maria's English (**1**) *is improving* (improve) every day. Three weeks ago she (**2**) .... (manage) to book us on to the Portsmouth to Santander ferry at the local travel agent's.

The night before we (**3**) .... (be) due to leave, she (**4**) .... (ring) me up to remind me to be on time. 'Don't forget the train (**5**) .... (leave) at 7.35 and if we (**6**) .... (miss) that, we (**7**) .... (miss) the ferry too!' she said.

'Of course I (**8**) .... (get) there on time,' I replied, somewhat annoyed. 'You're the one who (**9**) .... (always turn up) late for things!'

Surprisingly, we both (**10**) .... (arrive) at the station in time (**11**) .... (catch) the train. We (**12**) .... (sit) on the train for about ten minutes when we realised, to our horror, that it (**13**) .... (go) in the wrong direction! We got off at the next station where a ticket seller informed us that there (**14**) .... (not be) another train to Portsmouth until 8.45. We explained that we had to catch the ferry at 10 o'clock. 'Well, if I (**15**) .... (be) you,' he said, 'I (**16**) .... (catch) the coach. That should get you to Portsmouth before the ferry (**17**) .... (sail). But you (**18**) .... (have) to hurry, it (**19**) .... (leave) the bus station in about five minutes!'

We shot off like lightning despite the heavy rucksacks on our backs and jumped on the coach just as the driver (**20**) .... (shut) the doors. We (**21**) .... (just collapse) in our seats with a sigh of relief, when the driver announced, 'Sorry everyone but the motorway (**22**) .... (still repair) so we (**23**) .... (not get) to Portsmouth until 9.45.'

We groaned in despair. That gave us only fifteen minutes to get to the ferry terminal. We arrived at Portsmouth bus station at 9.40 and jumped straight into a taxi.

'The Santander ferry terminal and please hurry,' I shouted, 'or it (**24**) .... (go) before we (**25**) .... (get) there!'

To our astonishment, the taxi driver calmly switched off the engine and turned round.

'(**26**) .... you .... (not hear)?' he said, smiling, 'the ferry workers (**27**) .... (come) out on strike last night!'

'Oh no!' I cried in disbelief. 'If only I (**28**) .... (listen) to the news this morning!'

5 Writing – Report

Complete the report opposite based on the following notes. Use only one word in each space. Two examples are given for guidance.

- CD tried out by 30 intermediate level EFL students

- all completed brief feedback questionnaire

- 10 also interviewed in greater depth

- most liked the package – particularly chance to follow same lesson through different 'paths' i.e. grammar, pronunciation or vocabulary
  'I love following the vocabulary path.' Marina Gomez
  'My problem is pronunciation so I follow that path.' Kimiko Kamogawa
  'I need to know the grammar or I'm not happy.' Franz Brandt

- all liked the idea of personalised learning speed

- authors' worry that material was 'too low level' was unjustified

- some problems with pilot version – clicked on some buttons and nothing happened! → need for programmers to go through everything carefully

- main worry was over pronunciation strand – students couldn't really 'monitor' themselves and continued to make mistakes which they thought correct → possibility of inbuilding 'voice recognition' software?

- 17 students did not like the graphics → definitely needs to be reworked
  NB Most mentioned 'dull' colours

- users unfamiliar with computer mouse couldn't cope → need for optional introductory lesson on using PC?

Report on Boxhill Press 'Intermediate English CD ROM' (Pilot Version)

Introduction

The (1) *aim* of this report is to describe the reaction of (2) *thirty* individual students to the new 'Intermediate English CD ROM'. It is (3) .... on written (4) .... from all of the students and face-to face (5) .... with a representative number of them.

Positive notes

On the (6) .... , the students liked the CD package. (7) .... particular, they enjoyed being able to (8) .... their preferred 'path' through each unit. (9) .... to Franz Brandt, a German student, he wouldn't be happy unless he could follow the grammar path, (10) .... other students were happy to follow different paths. (11) .... , all students liked the fact that they could progress through the material at their (12) .... speed. (13) .... enough, the students all found the material sufficiently challenging at intermediate level.

Negative points

As might have been (14) .... , there were some technical problems with this pilot version. It (15) .... , for example, that several of the click boxes were inactive. In (16) .... to this, concern was expressed that less computer-literate users found mouse control difficult. More (17) .... , it was (18) .... by most students that the graphics were too dull. Perhaps an even greater (19) .... for concern at this stage is that it is impossible for students to effectively self-assess their performance on the pronunciation path.

Conclusions and recommendations

On (20) .... , it appears that Boxhill Press have produced a very promising product, which should soon establish itself as a market leader. (21) .... , it is strongly (22) .... that certain changes be made to the pilot version, (23) .... that the programmers ensure that all click-boxes are active, that Boxhill add an optional introductory lesson for the less computer-literate, that more vibrant colours be used in the graphics, and, most (24) .... , that Boxhill investigate the possibility of adding 'voice recognition' software to the CD to make the pronunciation path more effective for self-assessment.

6 Wordcheck – Studying and examinations

In the grid below there are 18 words connected with studying and taking exams: 7 are hidden horizontally, 7 vertically and 4 diagonally. When you have found them all, complete the sentences with some of them. Three have been found for you.

1 A student who enters for an exam is called a
....

2 It's a good idea to try and use some ....
aids when preparing for the exam.

3 Another verb meaning to take an examination is
....

4 Stretching and breathing exercises can help you keep
your exam .... under control.

5 Read all the .... carefully before attempting
to answer them and .... all your answers
before the end of the exam.

6 Most people try not only to .... the exam
but also to get a good ....

7 Be careful not to spend too long on one part of the
exam; remember there is a ....

8 Stay calm and try not to .... during the
exam as this can badly affect your ....

7 Editing skills

In most lines of the following text there is one word which is wrongly spelled, including the use of capital letters. <u>Underline</u> each wrongly spelled word and write the correct spelling in the space provided. If there are no spelling mistakes in a line, indicate this with a tick (✓). Look at the examples provided (0).

If you're going skiing this winter, here's a cautionary tale.	0 ✓
Last december three friends decided to go on a cheap skiing	0 *December*
holiday in the dolomites in the north of Italy. Being an	1 ....
adventureous lot, they decided to go by car, which turned out	2 ....
to be Dan's ancient VW Beetle. On the way there, they had no	3 ....
problems except for a little quarreling about whose turn it	4 ....
was to drive. The trouble started on there first day's skiing	5 ....
when Amy paniced, fell over and broke her ankle. On the	6 ....
second day, Charlie woke up saying, 'I think I'm dieing'.	7 ....
In fact, he had caught pneumonia. On the third day, Dan tryed	8 ....
to be too clever and broke a leg! All of this meant they	9 ....
payed plenty in doctor's bills and then, with nobody able to	10 ....
drive, they traveled back by plane and the car went back by	11 ....
train! So, all in all, it was an extremly expensive trip!	12 ....

 ▶ # Progress Test Four

Units 12–14

1 Structural cloze

For questions 1–15, complete the following story by writing each missing word in the space. Use only one word for each space. The exercise begins with an example (0).

Business affairs

Jeff Weaver knew it was going to be a tough meeting. A year ago he had been regarded (0) *as* the company's rising star in the export department, signing contracts for massive orders from state-run companies in Lavania. It looked as (1) .... he had saved the company's fortunes. But all that was before the collapse of the Lavanian economy and the inevitable non-payment of most invoices.

The Managing Director, Derek Robinson, had decided to (2) .... an extraordinary meeting (3) .... look into the matter. Jeff was now about to (4) .... asked to give a detailed explanation of the disaster.

Mr Robinson coughed and tapped the table. 'Right then, everyone. Let's get (5) .... to business. I'm sure you're all aware of the reasons for this meeting. So without further preamble, I'll call on Mr Weaver who, I hope, will be able to put our minds (6) .... rest about this worrying state of affairs.'

Jeff stood up and decided to go on the attack. 'Thank you, Mr Robinson. First of all, I must admit that many mistakes have been made over the past twelve months – but not just by me! I think it's clear that I am (7) .... used as a shield to protect a number of more senior colleagues, who (8) .... have the courage to assume some responsibility for this mess. In particular, my immediate superior, Georgina Bunyon, who has never seen eye (9) .... eye with me, and who is using this crisis (10) .... a way of (11) .... me removed from the company!'

Everyone turned to look at Georgina, who was (12) .... her fists and glaring pointedly at Jeff.

'No-one (13) .... have predicted the collapse of the Lavanian economy. However, to avoid further embarrassment, I have decided to resign.' And with this, Jeff marched out of the meeting.

Two months later, Jeff and Georgina were sitting looking at Lake Como from the terrace of a beautiful villa (14) .... they had just bought with part of what they called their 'Lavanian fund'.

'Any regrets, darling?' asked Georgina.

'Only one,' said Jeff, smiling. 'I (15) .... we'd taken twice as much!'

2 Phrasal verbs

Complete each of the following sentences with the appropriate form of a suitable phrasal verb. An example is shown.

Example: We all thought the lecture would be rather boring but it *turned out* to be extremely interesting.

1 As we didn't have an instructions manual, we had to .... how to set up the stereo by trial and error.
2 It's a formal occasion so we'll have to get .... to the nines – no jeans and pullovers this time!
3 Toby's .... really well at his new job. He's already been promoted twice.
4 Sarah's really lucky. She left her car in a no-parking area for five hours and, believe it or not, she .... with it!
5 Oh dear, Helen, your glass is almost empty. Let me .... it .... for you.

3 Register cloze

For questions 1–12, read the following memo from the Director of Studies to the new Health and Safety officer of a language school and use the information to complete the numbered gaps in the fire notice. Use no more than two words for each gap. The words you need do not occur in the memo. The exercise begins with an example (0).

Memorandum

To: David
From: Kim
RE: Fire notices for inspection next week

As you know, we've got the all-important inspection coming up next week and we still haven't got any proper fire notices up!
Can you put something official-looking together on the computer – don't forget to laminate the notices! Make sure you include the following:
• if you see/smell a fire, set off the nearest alarm
• try and put the fire out if you can but don't get burnt/trapped
• go to the meeting place (behind the library)
• wait for your name to be called out
• if you hear the alarm, get out straight away – don't try and pick up any books, coats, etc
• go to the meeting place but don't lose control or run
• don't go back into the building until the senior fire officer (that's you by the way!) says it's OK

Kim

FIRE NOTICE

On (0) *discovering* **a fire:**

1 (1) .... the nearest fire alarm
2 (2) .... to (3) .... the fire but (4) .... risks
3 Proceed to the (5) .... point (to the (6) .... the library)
4 (7) .... roll call

On hearing the fire alarm:

1 Leave without stopping to (8) ....
2 Proceed to the library quickly but without (9) .... or running
3 (10) .... outside the building until (11) .... that it is safe (12) .... by a senior fire officer

4 Error correction

In most lines of the following text there is one **unnecessary word**. It is either grammatically incorrect or does not fit in with the **sense of the text. For each** numbered line, find the unnecessary word and then **write it in the space** provided. Some lines are correct. Indicate these with a tick (✓). **The exercise** begins with two examples (0).

Note-taking

Obsessive note-taking which is the occupational hazard of
students. They believe they remember things best by writing them
down. Writing things down, however, it is still a practice that can
be abused as it can so easily lead back to a passive and
unconfident attitude to books; every little point the student
reads may in its context be so persuasive and that he feels
obliged to include it in his notes, which also become an abridged
version of the original. What the obsessive note-taker usually
postpones learning by understanding till he comes to read in his
notes; but as such these are not always the product of
understanding, they may be lengthy and unreliable. Furthermore,
reading sentence-by-sentence or paragraph-by-paragraph note-
taking commits the reader to further page-by-page reading; and as
we shall see later, this situation is not necessarily the best
way of reading slowly and understanding a book. The reader's
notes should be both the outcome of understanding and not
the prelude to it. Notes written of this kind are not only far
more briefer, but also better organised and more personalised.

0	*which*
0	✓
1	....
2	....
3	....
4	....
5	....
6	....
7	....
8	....
9	....
10	....
11	....
12	....
13	....
14	....
15	....
16	....

5 Lexical cloze

For questions 1–15, read the following passage carefully and decide which word best fits each space. The exercise begins with an example (0).

Lunatics

One of the oldest beliefs in folklore is that a full moon can (0) .B. a sane person into a madman. Robert Louis Stevenson's Dr Jekyll and Mr Hyde was (1) .... by the real-life activities of Charles Hyde, who (2) .... horrendous crimes during the full moon. In 1992, Christopher Gore began a sentence at Broadmoor hospital after being (3) .... of killing his parents. He is also (4) .... of killing two others – all four crimes (5) .... to nights of the full moon. Perhaps because of the enormous amount of anecdotal evidence from people working in the emergency services, some scientific research has been conducted in this (6) .... – but the conclusions are mixed. In 1972, research at the University of Miami seemed to show that the homicide rate in the city reached a (7) .... at each full moon. In India, there is much reported violent crime around the time of the full moon – but then the Indians are famously (8) .... in the full moon and ready to (9) .... misdemeanours on the moon's influence. 'Anecdotally, (10) .... nurses say patients become more disturbed when the moon is full, and firemen report more (11) .... of arson. Indeed, scientific research does show a correlation between changed behaviour and the full moon,' Dr David Nias, (12) .... in medical psychology at St Bartholomew's Hospital, London, admitted recently. 'However, this blip is explained by the small number of people who believe in the 'full moon effect' changing their behaviour accordingly – in much the same (13) .... as believers in astrology modify their behaviour to (14) .... that associated with their star (15) .... .

0	A make	B turn	C cause	D create
1	A based	B inspired	C founded	D exemplified
2	A made	B produced	C realised	D committed
3	A charged	B arrested	C convicted	D apprehended
4	A suspected	B involved	C believed	D implicated
5	A connected	B associated	C linked	D joined
6	A department	B range	C section	D field
7	A top	B peak	C tip	D summit
8	A fascinated	B obsessed	C interested	D attracted
9	A blame	B accuse	C explain	D refer
10	A psychotic	B psychopath	C psychic	D psychiatric
11	A episodes	B accidents	C cases	D events
12	A student	B teacher	C professor	D lecturer
13	A degree	B means	C way	D amount
14	A agree	B concur	C align	D match
15	A type	B name	C sign	D symbol

6 Word formation

For questions 1–15, read the two texts below. Use the words in the boxes to form one word that fits in the same numbered spaces in the texts. The exercise begins with an example (0).

Graphology

Graphology is the study of aspects of people's (0) *handwriting* to reveal their (1) .... A graphologist would claim to be able to (2) .... you by looking at such things as how you cross your 't's or dot your 'i's or whether your words slope backwards or forwards. Decreasing margins indicate (3) .... or subordination, whereas increasing margins show (4) .... Angular joins between letters are said to show strong will power and a certain (5) .... to adapt. Many people are, of course, quite (6) .... of graphology and its claims to 'read' people's characters. When compared with the results of established psychologists' tests, graphology has been shown to be generally (7) .... and a poor indicator of true character.

0	WRITE
1	PERSON
2	CATEGORY
3	SECURE
4	GENEROUS
5	ABLE
6	DISMISS
7	RELY

One good turn deserves another

On his way to the all-important job interview at St Cake's, Rupert had foolishly stopped to help someone fix an old car, which was barely (8) .... This meant he arrived late and had oil marks on his shirt and jacket. He went into reception and was led into a waiting room with great (9) .... There were three other candidates there, who (10) .... stared in amazement at his clothes. Clearly, the (11) .... rule was smile at no-one and speak to no-one! The other three were, of course, immaculately dressed and (12) .... cool, calm and collected. Rupert suddenly felt completely (13) .... as he imagined a (14) .... scene with the interviewers barely able to hide their contempt for him as he sat, dirty and sweating, on the chair in front of them! After thirty interminable minutes, Rupert was finally called into the interview room. As he entered, a familiar-looking old man greeted him, 'Ah, Mr Chester, the man with the in-depth (15) .... of the old Rover 80!' Rupert smiled. Maybe he would get the job after all!

8	ROAD
9	SOLEMN
10	REPEAT
11	SPEAK
12	SEEM
13	COURAGE
14	NIGHTMARE
15	KNOW

Answer Key ▶

1 ▶ Use Your Head

1.1 (Suggested answers only)

2 carefully, now   3 cat, house   4 but, moreover   5 hers, mine
6 information, luggage   7 cats, houses   8 tall, funny   9 sleep,
catch   10 was kidnapped, were arrested

1.2

1 adjective   2 verb   3 adverb   4 adverb   5 noun   6 adverb

1.3

2 's it going – present continuous   3 have you been waiting –
present perfect continuous   4 they will have finished – future
perfect simple   5 were you doing – past continuous   6 'll be
able – future simple   7 Had Julia ever been – past perfect
simple   8 'll have been working – future perfect continuous
9 've just had – present perfect simple   10 did you buy – past
simple   11 'll be sitting – future continuous   12 We had been
walking – past perfect continuous

1.4

2 to … about   3 in   4 on (about)   5 with   6 on   7 to   8 with
9 to   10 with

2.1

2 broke down/ran out of petrol   3 wash   4 you work
5 (should) see him   6 will we get to   7 I have   8 I'd slap
9 you use/look after it   10 lands   11 I spoke/could speak
12 you require (any)   13 it gets/turns   14 wouldn't get/have
15 there are/you have   16 you were shipwrecked/stranded
17 I were/was   18 it rains/'s raining   19 you be/find yourself
20 didn't (always) have

2.2

2 Although F   3 I but   4 Although H   5 Despite/In spite of J
6 A despite/in spite of   7 Although C   8 In spite G   9 B in
spite   10 Despite/In spite of E

3.1

2 OK   3 think it over   4 OK   5 look through this article
6 put it off   7 OK   8 put it down   9 OK   10 give it up

3.2

2 for it   3 it out/away   4 after him   5 it up   6 it back   7 it up
8 to it   9 it over/about it   10 it in/out   11 it out   12 over it
13 it up   14 them up   15 her round

4.1

2 underestimate, overestimate   3 understate, overstate
4 undernourished, overnourished   5 undercharge, overcharge
6 understaffed, overstaffed   7 undercooked (underdone),
overcooked (overdone)   8 underdressed, overdressed
9 underuse, overuse   10 underprivileged, overprivileged   11
underrate, overrate   12 underexpose, overexpose

4.2

2 overdressed   3 undersized   4 overstatement
5 underestimate   6 overstaffed   7 underused   8 overestimate
9 underdone/undercooked   10 overrated   11 understatement
12 undernourished   13 overcharge   14 underprivileged

6   Layout and style mistakes

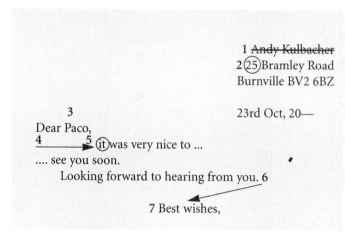

Missing phrases:
1 hear from you   2 I was/am glad   3 I wonder (was
wondering) if I could ask/I need (want) to ask you a   4 I'd be
(terribly/really/very) grateful   5 hesitate to say no/worry
6 Anyway   7 Hope to/I hope to

6

3 beneficial   4 complexity   5 intellectual   6 misconception
7 deceitful   8 anxiety   9 dishonest   10 explanation
11 photographic   12 inattentive   13 psychological
14 investment   15 disappearance   16 deceitful … dishonest
17 misconception   18 explanation … disappearance
19 beneficial … psychological   20 anxiety   21 inattentive …
photographic   22 complexity   23 intellectual   24 efficiency

7

2 assimilate   3 undergo   4 reported   5 jot down   6 set
yourself   7 parroting   8 prove   9 offer   10 chewing over
11 produce   12 circulated

8.1

2 an (indefinite article)   3 The (definite article)   4 can (modal
verb)   5 been (be)   6 to (preposition)   7 which (relative
pronoun)   8 the (definite article)   9 which (relative pronoun)
10 into (preposition)

8.2

1 ✓   2 that   3 in   4 that   5 of   6 When   7 have   8 ✓
9 ✓   10 of   11 ✓   12 ✓   13 up   14 the

2 ▶ Severe Weather

1.1

2 I 3 H 4 F 5 J 6 A 7 C 8 G 9 B 10 D

1.2

2 foggiest 3 stormy 4 sunny 5 storms 6 showering 7 hail
8 frosty 9 floods 10 cloud

2

2 while/whereas 3 yet 4 in contrast/on the other hand
5 while/whereas 6 but 7 while/whereas 8 Although

3

2 standstill 3 hold 4 advantage 5 hint 6 give 7 role

4

2 on … stand-by 3 warned … against 4 admission of
5 under … illusions 6 cleared of 7 into action 8 increase in
9 to tears 10 fitted with

5 (Model answer)

> 10 North Parade
> Loxley
>
> 15 April 20—
>
> The Chairman
> Town Council
> Loxley
>
> Dear Sir,
>
> I am writing to express my concern about the appalling
> state of the road outside my house. Indeed, the road is in
> such bad repair that my nextdoor neighbour recently had
> the misfortune to get the back wheel of her car stuck in
> one of the enormous potholes outside my gate. She was
> not only most distressed by the incident but also had to
> pay for a breakdown truck to pull her car out.
>
> The damage to the road surface is clearly the result of the
> period of extremely cold weather we had with ice and
> snow. That, however, was two months ago and still
> nothing has been done, despite the fact that the road was
> inspected by a member of the council immediately after
> the weather improved.
>
> I must, therefore, insist that the council takes steps to
> have the road repaired as soon as possible. Moreover, I
> must urge the council to take appropriate action to
> ensure that situations like this are rectified more
> promptly in the future.
>
> I look forward to hearing from you.
>
> Yours faithfully,
>
> Fred Smith

6

2 OK or aging 3 studying 4 swimming 5 OK 6 dying
7 kidnapped 8 OK 9 paid 10 tried 11 arguing 12 referred
13 played 14 OK 15 panicked

7.1

2 both possible (got – more probable) 3 was (only) 4 getting
(only) 5 be (only) 6 both possible 7 Get (only) 8 get
(only) 9 get (only) 10 both possible

7.2

2 be required 3 be accompanied by a cheque guarantee card
4 is not allowed inside the cathedral 5 should be addressed to
the manager 6 will be notified before the end of the month
7 should be received within ten working days 8 has not been
granted 9 will be paid (if) for money (is) lost in the post
10 must be accompanied by an adult

8

2 into 3 back 4 off 5 about 6 into 7 into 8 by
9 from … to 10 to

9

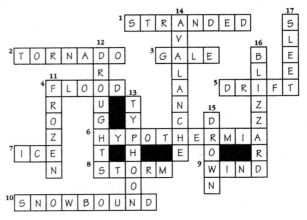

3 ▶ Time Eaters

1.1

2 informal, fat/overweight 3 informal, mad/crazy/insane
4 formal, write 5 dated, radio 6 legal, stealing/theft
7 informal, quite/rather/somewhat 8 dated, go out with
9 formal, despite (the fact or thing mentioned) 10 informal,
large meal 11 formal, wise/prudent 12 informal, trick/deceive
13 medical, collar bone 14 informal, language

1.2

2 collar bone 3 Language 4 meal/dinner 5 OK 6 despite
7 somewhat 8 Overweight 9 OK 10 write 11 OK
12 going out (together) 13 cuts 14 stealing

2

2 B how much 3 H which 4 A what 5 how C 6 when I
7 what E 8 J how 9 G who 10 D whose

3.1

2 'll have (have also possible)   3 're going to crash   4 'll have
5 'll get   6 isn't/'s not going to rain   7 'm just going to stay
8 probably won't remember   9 'll get   10 'm going to sneeze

3.2

2 As soon as/When/Once   3 until   4 After   5 while   6 if
7 When/Once/As soon as   8 until   9 By the time
10 Once/When/As soon as

3.3 (Suggested answers only)

2 you've finished   3 you're seeing the bank manager   4 we get
there   5 've finished the exam   6 you leave the car here   7 go
to bed   8 has worn off

3.4

2 're forever using   3 know   4 's going   5 leaves   6 's writing
7 always gives   8 doesn't seem, 's always leaving   9 're having
10 rescues, gets   11 are you living   12 serves, returns, goes

3.5

2 be able to come   3 must have taken   4 might have left
5 could/might/may have got   6 could swim   7 was able to
swim   8 could/might/may have told   9 couldn't find   10 be
able to run, can't even run   11 mightn't/can't have realised
12 can cause   13 couldn't have been   14 Can you see,
might/could/may well be   15 could have been   16 can't be
17 hasn't been able to hear   18 might/may bite

4 ▶ Stress

1

2 C result   3 H caused   4 K result   5 effect D   6 F
source/cause   7 L cause   8 result E   9 result A   10 G because
11 J lead   12 B due

2.1 (Suggested answers only)

2 Driving carelessly   3 Listening to the radio   4 Watching TV
5 Living abroad   6 Doing   7 Swimming   8 Reading   9 Having
a bath   10 Biting your nails

2.2

2 of going   3 of stealing   4 about accepting   5 in doing   6 at
taking   7 about seeing   8 for inviting   9 for breaking   10 of
seeing   11 in going   12 for forgetting   13 of telling   14 by
pressing   15 after coming   16 for getting   17 while/when
operating/using   18 while taking   19 In spite of eating
20 before overtaking

2.3

2 drinking   3 seeing   4 to cut   5 working, having   6 to realise
7 telling   8 to tell   9 to win   10 relying/depending, to stand
11 to pass, playing   12 wondering, coming/getting
13 worrying, to know   14 smoking, breathing   15 being, to
smash   16 to take, fixing/repairing/adjusting   17 risking,
getting, leaving/parking   18 promising, to help, getting

2.4

2 showing   3 following   4 sightings   5 airing   6 reading
7 saying   8 carving   9 setting   10 awakening   11 hearing
12 spellings   13 beings   14 fittings   15 recording

2.5

2 K   3 J   4 A/O   5 H   6 L   7 E   8 M   9 D   10 N   11 B   12 C
13 O/A   14 F   15 I

3

2 enlarge   3 smarten   4 popularised   5 purify   6 summarise
7 endangers   8 cannibalised   9 horrified   10 lengthening
11 clarify   12 lessen   13 enforce   14 terrorising
15 heightened

4

2 in – for   3 with – in   4 through – over   5 at – to   6 with –
in   7 in – on   8 on – into   9 at – in   10 for – on

5

2 meet   3 modify   4 provide   5 answer   6 calm, doing   7 take
8 receive   9 organise   10 attends

6.1

2 rush   3 dizzy   4 mull over   5 focus   6 result   7 vulnerable
8 boosted

6.2

2 E   3 F   4 J   5 H   6 I   7 A   8 D   9 G   10 B

Progress Test One

1

1 which   2 as   3 over   4 Having   5 going   6 spite
7 While/As   8 who   9 would/might   10 without   11 good
12 where   13 matter   14 queuing   15 until   16 apologising
17 understaffed   18 result   19 under   20 unless/although

2

1 lead to   2 ringing up/phoning up   3 weigh up   4 let …
down   5 rounded off/finished off

3

1 being   2 not   3 ✓   4 for   5 so   6 ✓   7 with   8 ✓   9 as
10 When   11 up   12 ✓   13 ✓   14 the   15 are   16 it

4

1 intensified   2 torrential   3 dreadful   4 sleepless
5 endless/unending   6 safety   7 desperate   8 overworked
9 ailments   10 ineffective   11 undergo   12 particularly
13 recognition   14 scientifically   15 harmless

5

1 H   2 A   3 F   4 E   5 B   6 D

5 ▶ Globe Trotting

as soon as/immediately/once   3 As well as/In addition to
Owing/Due to   5 during   6 Since/As   7 OK   8 so that
OK   10 delete however   11 OK   12 in order to/so as to/to

.1

was living, met   3 Weren't you working, had   4 got, became
heard, was going   6 went, left   7 lived, were always having
was hoping   9 was living, was published   10 saw, was
owing, were gathering   11 were lying, was working   12 rang,
icked, put   13 never understood, always got   14 worked,
ent   15 was, always went, really loved, often rained

.2

turned up   3 explained   4 had been held up   5 didn't find
had been blowing   7 (had) called   8 was lying   9 had been
riving   10 (had) appeared   11 (had) braked   12 (had)
kidded   13 (had) managed   14 was filling up   15 was
earing   16 had tied   17 was pulling   18 opened   19 jumped
0 had swum

.1

brush up   3 drink up   4 do up   5 split/break up   6 round
p   7 made up   8 gang up   9 look it up   10 speed up

.2

looked on to   3 dropped off to   4 build up   5 taken aback
pulled up   7 stubbed out   8 go through with   9 pull out
0 started up   11 pulled over   12 jumped out of   13 shot off
4 pulled … off   15 ripped off

.3

away with   3 up to   4 up with   5 forward to   6 up on   7 off
ith   8 out for   9 on with   10 round to

[4]

G The latter   3 A such   4 H the above   5 F this   6 C which
B Another   8 E that

hostess, take-off   3 check in   4 Lavatories   5 terminal
boarding card   7 standby   8 delay, take off

6 (Corrected mistakes numbered and shown in bold)

5 Redland Road
Barford BF2 8VR
21st May 20–

Randolph Jefferies
20 The Green
Hinton
Devon HN3 2CC

Dear (1) **Mr Jefferies**

I was most interested (2) **in** your advertisement (3) **in** 'The Independent' and I am writing (4) **to obtain further** (5) **information** about your country cottage holidays.

In particular, I would like (6) **to know** in which parts of the country your cottages are located as my friends and I are interested (7) **in staying** as far away from large cities as possible. I would (8) **also** like to know if it would be possible (9) **to rent** a cottage for six people for up to six months and whether pets are allowed as my friends and I have three well-behaved dogs we are planning to take with us.

I should, therefore, be (10) **most/extremely/terribly** grateful if you (11) **would** send me full details of your larger, more isolated cottages and any brochures you may have.
Thanking you in advance for your help. I look forward to (12) **hearing** from you as (13) **soon** as possible.

Yours (14) **sincerely,**

Sandy Melville

7

0 paid   1 ✓   2 ✓   3 (give) up   4 (turned) out   5 ✓
6 turned (out)   7 (sorted) out   8 ✓   9 (making) for
10 ✓   11 ✓   12 ✓   13 ✓   14 (stick) to   15 (write) off   16 ✓

8

2 shrugged   3 hiding   4 take   5 way   6 lead   7 soul
8 promote   9 tongue   10 put

6 ▶ Language Matters

1.1

2 OK 3 Isn't that the hotel Greg and Sally had their wedding reception in? 4 The gentleman you spoke to last time is no longer with the company. 5 OK 6 OK 7 The reason the accident happened has never been clarified. 8 Is this the picture you were referring to? 9 OK 10 That's the car we were thinking of buying.

1.2

1b whose mayor was arrested for corruption? c which/that was almost completely destroyed during the war? d where Richard Burton was born? 2a whose author I can never remember the name of? b which/that was reviewed in *The Times* last week? c (which/that) I lent you last term? 3a who lived in China until she was 16? b (who/that) the restaurant sacked for being rude to customers? c whose boyfriend wants to go and live in Italy? 4a (which/that) you wanted to have off? b which/that had to be invented to make the year longer? c when most people get married?

1.3

2 yes 3 no 4 yes 5 yes 6 no 7 no 8 no 9 yes 10 yes

1.4

2 taken back/brought back/returned 3 cooked in 4 given/treated with 5 left/allowed 6 booked by/reserved by 7 taken/stolen/removed, parked/left in 8 dug up at (on)/found at (on)/discovered at (on)/unearthed at (on) 9 washed in/with 10 painted 11 brought into/imported into 12 left

2

2 as 3 alike, like 4 as 5 alike 6 like 7 As 8 like

3.1

2 so/as intelligent as 3 better 4 the most carefully 5 as/so mountainous a country as 6 most northern/most northerly/northernmost 7 as much time … as 8 as careful a driver as 9 more frequently than 10 the heaviest

3.2

2 C 3 F 4 J 5 H 6 E 7 K 8 I 9 D 10 L 11 A 12 B

3.3

2 as blind as a bat 3 as flat as a pancake 4 as dry as a bone 5 as fresh as a daisy 6 as slippery as an eel 7 as weak as a kitten 8 as stubborn as a mule 9 as thin as a rake 10 as proud as a peacock 11 as strong as an ox 12 as deaf as a post

4 (Some variations are possible)

2 slightly older than 3 exactly half as much as 4 much more than 5 a little/slightly shorter than 6 slightly taller than 7 three times as many hours per day as 8 slightly fewer hours per day than 9 about half as much (money) as 10 over five times as much (money) as 11 a great deal more exercise than 12 slightly less exercise than

5

2 Not only, but also 3 Moreover/Furthermore 4 In addition to/As well as/Besides 5 as if/as though 6 Although/Even though/Though 7 Even if 8 yet 9 in spite of/despite 10 However 11 nevertheless 12 whereas/while

6.2

1 stopped 2 patrolling 3 studying 4 debatable 5 forgetting 6 OK 7 happier 8 OK 9 accommodation 10 doubtful

7

2 OK 3 absolutely/completely/totally 4 very/extremely 5 OK 6 absolutely/completely/totally 7 very/extremely 8 OK 9 OK 10 absolutely/completely/totally

8

1 A 2 D 3 C 4 B 5 A 6 D 7 B 8 C 9 A 10 A 11 B 12 D 13 C 14 B 15 C

7 ▶ The Ages of Man

1.1

2 I used to (play) 3 B 'm used to 4 J got used to 5 C 'd been used to being 6 G didn't use to 7 A to get used to 8 H wasn't used to working 9 F used to drink it 10 D get used to obeying

1.2

2 did you live 3 took, was 4 didn't live 5 's happened, 've seen 6 wrote, was 7 did you buy 8 've seen 9 Did you ever steal, were 10 has been 11 went, did you think 12 did you get 13 witnessed, happened 14 's broken 15 smoked, gave up, hasn't touched

1.3

2 did you see, haven't seen 3 've been learning, for 4 did you live 5 Has … finished, has just been published 6 've been living, since, got 7 have you had 8 Have you been suffering, for 9 haven't repaired 10 hasn't won 11 've taken, did 12 Has Maisy phoned, said 13 have you eaten 14 've been using, since, haven't found 15 's been eating, since

1.4

2 'm thinking 3 don't think 4 looks 5 definitely smells 6 tastes 7 realise 8 'm not feeling/don't feel 9 doesn't surprise 10 seem 11 remember 12 need 13 'm seeing 14 suppose 15 promise

2.1

1 with a lot of hair, neutral 2 dangerous, negative 3 amusing, positive 4 strange, negative 5 pleasant, positive 6 small, neutral

2.2

7 noun 8 adverb 9 adjective 10 adjective

2.3

11 hard-headed = practical and unemotional when making difficult decisions

12 hard luck = expression of commiseration when someone fails in something
13 hard up = not having enough money to buy essential things
14 doesn't exist – hard headed
15 hard nut = informal expression for someone who is physically or mentally very strong (or thinks they are)
16 doesn't exist – hard of hearing
17 doesn't exist – heavy sleeper
18 doesn't exist – hard liquor
19 hard cash = money in notes or coins, not cheques or credit cards
20 hard-hearted = not caring about other people's feelings

2.4
21 G   22 I   23 B   24 H   25 C   26 D   27 E   28 J   29 A   30 F
Verbs not needing to add the part of the body: 21 wink
23 nod   24 shrug   29 pout   30 clap

2.5
31 useless   32 usable   33 used   34 usefully   35 Users

2.6
36 buoy   37 wrestling   38 knick-knack   39 comb   40 sword
41 guitar   42 photographer   43 difficulty   44 calculator
45 original

3   (Some variations are possible)
2 Colin promised he'd/to repair the back door last/that weekend.
3 Karen admitted she'd scratched the car.   4 Maurice threatened to tell the police if they didn't give/unless they gave him £5,000.
5 Hilary insisted that I go/went to Dave's party with her on Saturday.   6 Silvia mentioned that Terry's house was still for sale.   7 Mr Penfold swore he'd never seen the money before.
8 The mountain guide warned them not to go walking in the fog (because it could be dangerous).   9 He couldn't remember if it was Leonardo or Michelangelo who painted/had painted the Mona Lisa.   10 Julian announced/told us/informed us that he and Nina were getting married the following year.   11 Jemima boasted/claimed she was the best tennis player at the college.   12 Dr Bianchi asked Dr McPherson if (s)he'd mind repeating the question/to repeat his/her question.   13 George complained that the service in the restaurant was incredibly slow.   14 The shop assistant suggested it might be better to/that I (should) wait until the manager got there.   15 The doctor advised Jack to eat less and take more exercise.

4
2 time do you make it?   3 would make   4 make it   5 do you make it?   6 're going to/'ll make it?

5
1 C   2 F   3 G   4 A   5 I

6
2 toddler   3 stamina   4 middle-aged   5 teenager   6 seventies
7 prodigy   8 infant   9 early   The hidden word: longevity

8 ▶ Personally Speaking

1
2 big-headed   3 broad-minded   4 thin-skinned   5 tight-fisted
6 level-headed   7 short-tempered

2   (* = Suggested answer only)
2 more/less interesting, more/less likely   3 less easy/easier, more/less highly   4 more wine, less clearly   5 closer, *more nervous   6 more humid, worse   7 farther/further, *thicker
8 *The harder something is to do   9 *the less they practise their English   10 *The more stressful the situation

3
2 tick … off   3 put down   4 face up to   5 worked out   6 steer away from   7 eked out   8 fight … out   9 fall back on
10 picking out

4.1
2 is spread/put F   3 was invented D   4 will be/will have been wiped out/eradicated L   5 used to be/were extracted/taken out/pulled out J   6 could be bought/obtained I   7 should not be exposed B   8 was/used to be spoken C   9 has been/is simplified K   10 are used A   11 are being destroyed E   12 are regarded H

4.2
2 will probably be sent   3 will be/are taken   4 have already been picked   5 be picked   6 were sprayed   7 to be gathered
8 are harvested   9 are both made   10 to be made   11 is treated
12 are just shaken   13 is collected   14 (is) put   15 will be automated

4.3 (Suggested answers only)
2 to die   3 play on the grass   4 to have more accidents
5 realise how bad the situation really was   6 to give up smoking   7 to open his suitcase   8 leave the room   9 to learn to speak the language   10 lose my temper.

5
2 I was/am glad to hear you had a good time – apart from the sunburn!
3 I hope you've got over it and are feeling better (by) now.
4 Anyway, the reason (why) I'm writing is that Kim and I are having a party on Saturday 19th to celebrate the end of our exams.
5 I know it's rather a long way (for you) to come but I was wondering if/whether you'd like to stay the whole weekend.
6 We both hope you'll be able to make it.
7 Can you let me know if you're coming (or not) by next Friday?
8 Hope to hear from you soon.

6
2 restless (the others describe someone with a strong desire to do something)   3 impatient (the others describe someone who is not aware of or doesn't care about other people's feelings)
4 diligent (the others describe someone who communicates

well with other people) 5 calm (the others describe someone who finds it difficult to talk to other people) 6 carefree (the others describe someone who concentrates so as not to make mistakes) 7 charming (the others describe someone who feels/is feeling pleasure) 8 dynamic (the others describe someone you can place your faith in or trust)

7

1 C 2 D 3 C 4 A 5 C 6 B 7 C 8 D 9 B 10 A 11 B 12 D 13 B 14 C 15 A

Progress Test Two

I

1 for 2 much/far 3 used 4 able 5 while 6 long 7 like 8 do 9 bit/little 10 must 11 been 12 would 13 managed 14 coming 15 as

2

1 turned out 2 stood by 3 handed down 4 singles out 5 stick to

3

1 seaside 2 surprisingly 3 standby 4 twice 5 poorly 6 linguistically 7 farther/further 8 useless 9 defensive 10 restless 11 talkative 12 depth 13 sensitivity 14 unfeeling 15 resistance

4

1 too/as well 2 over/at least 3 been driving 4 put/write 5 about 6 cover/pay for 7 get 8 piece 9 get/hire/rent/pay for 10 cost

5

1 D 2 B 3 C 4 A 5 B 6 C 7 D 8 B 9 A 10 B 11 B 12 C 13 D 14 A 15 C

6

1 E 2 H 3 I 4 C 5 G 6 B

9 ▶ Mind Your Manners

I

2 Hardly had she stubbed out one cigarette when she lit another. 3 Not a soul did we see all day. 4 No sooner did/had I put the phone down than it rang again. 5 So quietly did he speak that I didn't hear a thing he said. 6 Not a (single) game did they win all season. 7 Such is life. 8 Only after she'd been speaking to him for ten minutes did she realise who he was. 9 Not only did Kate spill wine on the carpet, but she also broke six glasses. 10 Never (before) had I seen such a gigantic fish!

2

2 may leave 3 didn't have to change 4 needn't have rushed 5 must have/have to have/need to have 6 Can/Could/May/Might I ask 7 will be allowed/able to travel 8 should/ought to/must have 9 'll have to ask 10 don't have (need) to do/needn't do 11 to be allowed/able to build, can't put 12 Need we discuss/Do we need to discuss 13 should have kept 14 'll be allowed/able to build 15 weren't allowed to/couldn't make, had to use

3.1

2 promise 3 hold 4 experience 5 jokes 6 does 7 question/point 8 give 9 ease 10 date 11 priority 12 pay 13 made 14 blunder 15 move

3.2

2 uproariously 3 categorically 4 deeply 5 profusely 6 bitterly 7 heartedly 8 bitterly 9 warmly 10 flatly

3.3

2 prior engagement 3 kind invitation 4 unkind remark 5 distant relative 6 warm welcome 7 wedding reception 8 social climber 9 fond farewell 10 firm handshake, sunny smile 11 family get-together 12 close friend 13 relaxed atmosphere 14 candle-lit dinner

4.1

2 immobile 3 irrational 4 uncomfortable 5 non-smoker 6 irrelevant 7 unreliable 8 disrespect 9 insoluble 10 misbehave 11 illogical 12 discomfort 13 misspell 14 impolite 15 illegible 16 non-resident

4.2

17 rude – polite 18 clever/intelligent – stupid/unintelligent 19 thin – plump/fat 20 useful/convenient – useless/inconvenient

4.3

1 /ʌ/ 2 /ɔ:/ 3 /ɪ/ 4 /æ/ 5 /ɒ/ 6 /ɜ:/ 7 /u:/ 8 /ɑ:/

4.4

9 D 10 S 11 S 12 D 13 D 14 D 15 S 16 D 17 D 18 D

4.5

/ʌf/	/ə/	/aʊ/	/əʊ/
rough	thorough	bough	though
enough	borough	drought	dough
tough		plough	

/ɔ:/	/ɒf/	/u:/
thought	cough	through
nought	trough	

5

2 Jane would have applied for that job in the City if she had lived anywhere near/nearer London.
3 If Louis hadn't mentioned it to me in passing, I wouldn't have found out.
4 If a detective hadn't recognised him from an identikit picture, Ronald wouldn't be in prison.
5 Harry wouldn't have beaten me at tennis if he hadn't cheated/been such a terrible cheat!
6 If you hadn't left the map in the car, we wouldn't be lost!

We might have been able to fix the car when it broke down if
e had known anything about engines.
I would have prepared something special if I'd known they
ere coming.

(Model answer)

Report on the new 'Bambo' pushchair

Introduction
The aim of this report is to find out how good the new
'Bambo' pushchair is. It is based on interviews with 150
mothers and fathers in six different cities all over Britain.

Observations and comments
It was found that the majority of people interviewed had a
very favourable overall impression of the pushchair. In the
words of a Mrs Long of Gloucester, comparing it with her
old pushchair, 'The "Bambo" is fantastic – it's so light and
manageable' and as a Mr Blair of London said, it must be
comfortable as his little boy 'really likes going out in it'. On
the whole, most people interviewed agree the 'Bambo' has
the following good points: it is light and easy to steer; it is
good for carrying shopping on the tray under the baby's
seat; it is colourful and attractive to look at; the baby seems
comfortable as (s)he has 4 different positions ranging from
lying flat to sitting upright; it is easy to transport as it takes
up very little room when folded. There were, however,
some negative comments, which were: the opening hinge is
often stiff making it difficult to unfold; the wheels
themselves are rather small, which means the pushchair
often gets stuck in holes on uneven or rough ground; the
wheel locking mechanism on the back wheels is too small
to be operated by using one's foot, which means one has to
bend down to lock it by hand.

Recommendations
It is advisable for 'Bocia' to make the following changes to
their current model of 'Bambo' pushchair: a) make the
opening hinge easier to operate, b) increase the size of the
wheels, c) make the wheel locking mechanism large enough
to be operated by foot.

Conclusion
To sum up, the current model is already well established as
one of the best pushchairs on the market. However, acting
on the recommendations stated above, 'Bocia' should be
able to improve the product still further and possibly
become market leader.

7
1 Punctuality 2 serious 3 childish 4 poor state
5 repairs/maintenance 6 resources 7 location/position
8 inaccessible 9 furniture 10 stale/not fresh 11 supply
12 variety 13 bland 14 poorly 15 impolite 16 advance

10 ▶ State of the Union

1.1
2 seeing 3 have 4 to know 5 shouting 6 give
7 understanding 8 do 9 to have 10 to get

1.2
2 it's onions 3 the place/country 4 job satisfaction is
what/it's job satisfaction 5 The reason (why) 6 The man
7 It was the Dutch 8 the film we wanted to see 9 Wasn't it
10 the language spoken

2
2 have … party 3 make … commitment 4 the/that argument
we had 5 got engaged 6 do … ironing 7 gets … way
8 having … cry 9 making … sense 10 do … share

3
2 falling out 3 make up 4 break/split up 5 cheating on
6 asking/inviting … out 7 stood … up 8 get over 9 goes for
10 go off

4
2 in 3 on 4 of 5 with 6 towards 7 with 8 in 9 between
10 about

5 (Model answer)

Don't let your child's make-believe turn to tragedy!

Every year, hundreds of kids under the age of 5 are taken to hospital after swallowing something poisonous. Half of these children need to be kept in hospital. Some are accidentally poisoned when they think they are eating or drinking something nice.

MOST OF THESE ACCIDENTS ARE AVOIDABLE!

Safety checks you can make.
- Keep all medicines in a locked cabinet – or store them out of reach of children.
- Fit safety locks on the cupboard where you keep cleaning materials – including dishwasher and washing powder.
- Teach your kids to act safely – not to eat pills or berries and not to drink from a bottle unless a grown-up says it's OK.
- Be aware of plants and berries in your garden – find out which ones are harmful if eaten.

If your child has swallowed something harmful ...

Keep calm and read this panel carefully. If in doubt, phone **01742 313272**
- Do not make your child vomit
- Immediately call the Accident and Emergency department of your nearest hospital or take your child there directly
- Take the substance, plant or berries you think your child has swallowed with you

At the hospital the staff will need to know:
- How many tablets or berries your child may have swallowed
- When he/she took them
- Whether your child has any symptoms (eg vomiting)

STAY CALM BUT ACT QUICKLY

6

1 to 2 or 3 are 4 other 5 in 6 with 7 nor 8 like 9 on
10 often/frequently 11 that 12 these 13 instance/example
14 their 15 may

7

1 limited/limiting 2 production 3 Action 4 enjoyment
5 household 6 predictable 7 unemotional 8 primarily
9 contentedly 10 reliable 11 warning 12 discomfort
13 unable 14 considerably 15 brainwave

8

2 lonely-hearts 3 agony aunt 4 bride, groom 5 reception 6 honeymoon 7 confirmed bachelor 8 old flame 9 widower
10 marital status 11 Spouse 12 heart-throb

11 ▶ Last Chance to See

1.1

2 no commas 3 OK 4 no commas 5 OK 6 comma before *which* 7 comma before *which* 8 comma before *which* and after *chimpanzees* 9 OK 10 comma before *whose* and after *dog*

1.2

2 OK 3 The vegetation on which these animals depend is under threat. 4 There's that pen you've been looking for.
5 OK 6 ... 'Ginger' was the name he was generally known by.
7 But that chap we bought the car from said it was guaranteed!
8 The process by which the vast majority of nuclear power is produced is known as 'fission'. 9 OK 10 Those kids she looks after are really terrible!

2.1

2 cut up 3 dip into 4 holding ... up 5 carrying out
6 sprung up 7 make up 8 cut down

2.2

2 cut down 3 made up 4 make up 5 was held up 6 dip into
7 hold up 8 sprang up

3

2 will have finished 3 gets, 'll have 4 's going to fall 5 is due to open, 'll have been completed 6 is to/is due to/is going to give/is giving 7 'll have been living 8 'll be 9 doesn't start, 'll have 10 's going to have /'s having 11 'll be flying 12 'll phone 13 'll have finished 14 Shall I give, is Fred going to take/will Fred be taking/is Fred taking 15 're about to/going to close

4

2 ... both (of them) have ... 3 Neither 4 £1 each (one)
5 ... they both lead ... 6 OK 7 ... I know (very) few words ...
8 Each/Every student ... 9 OK or Every CD ... 10 ... seems little point ... 11 ... but neither of them ... 12 OK or ... all of them 13 ... for a few close friends ... 14 OK 15 OK

5

2 so that/in order that 3 in case 4 due to/owing to/as a result of/because of 5 As/Since/Because 6 so ... that 7 so 8 such ... that 9 consequently/therefore/as a result 10 As soon as/When/Once 11 until/till 12 Before 13 Hardly ... when or No sooner ... than 14 First, Then/Next/After that, Finally 15 While

6

2 166 High Street 3 in applying 4 post/position of 5 was advertised/I saw advertised 6 My reason for 7 have worked/been working 8 interested in/looking for 9 offer/give me
10 of working 11 to attend an 12 convenient 13 I look forward to hearing from you. 14 Yours sincerely, 15 OLIVIA JAMES

7

1 F 2 B 3 A 4 H 5 D

8

2 lead-free petrol 3 conservation policy 4 forest fire 5 rare species 6 Illegal poaching 7 long lifespan 8 logging rights
9 natural habitat 10 national parks

Progress Test Three

1
1 persuaded/convinced 2 when 3 make 4 how 5 do
6 until 7 which/that 8 which/that 9 harder/tougher
10 causing 11 what 12 While 13 After
14 meantime/meanwhile 15 sooner

2
1 carries out 2 gone out 3 broke out 4 send off 5 cut off

3
1 have been hung/are hung 2 have calmed 3 contains
4 hunt 5 makes the elks avoid 6 excited 7 are caused
8 OK 9 will be cut 10 costs 11 OK 12 was invented
13 stops elks eating 14 OK 15 would soon become 16 fear

4
1 E 2 B 3 H 4 A 5 G 6 D

5
1 painful 2 incorrect 3 childhood 4 accomplishments
5 unappreciated 6 inadequacy 7 unnecessary
8 behaviour 9 incomprehensible 10 unfriendly
11 uninterested 12 apologetic 13 embarrassment
14 impolite 15 inoffensive

12 ▶ Living Dangerously

1
2 hands 3 expose 4 reckless 5 dicing 6 adventure
7 blackspot 8 hand 9 daredevil 10 narrow 11 fire 12 neck
13 corner 14 ice 15 den

2
2 The thing I'd really like to try is bungee-jumping.
3 Inexperience not recklessness is the greatest cause of accidents.
4 Nowhere in the entire hotel was there a fire escape!
5 Under no circumstances must visitors approach the cages.
6 What most young people need is a sense of danger in their lives.
7 Not a living soul did we see for over two months!
8 It was not until three days after the accident that they were rescued.
9 No sooner had she left hospital than she went sky-diving again!
10 The rush of adrenalin is what I really love when I go skiing.

3.1
2 put … down to 3 brought out 4 cut off 5 put out 6 get over 7 broke out 8 cut off

3.2
2 got over 3 put … down to 4 cut … off 5 got over
6 broke out 7 put out 8 brings out

4
2 OK 3 … had never seen … 4 … has Dr Harris examined
… 5 … did you buy … 6 … worked … 7 I've written …
8 … had already started … 9 OK 10 I had been sitting …
11 OK 12 … had been snowing … 13 … has crashed …
14 … were riding … 15 … has been raining …

5.1
2 would still be living, hadn't found 3 hadn't looked, wouldn't have spotted 4 would ever have guessed, hadn't been caught
5 would never have got, hadn't been/gone 6 had taken, might/would be living 7 hadn't noticed, would be 8 would have been, hadn't lost 9 wouldn't be, hadn't known 10 'd listened, wouldn't be sitting

5.2
2 If we hadn't got soaking wet on Sunday, we wouldn't (all) have colds (now).
3 If I knew, I'd tell you.
4 I wouldn't have caught/managed to catch the train if it hadn't been 10 minutes late.
5 We'll have to cancel the barbecue if the weather's bad on Sunday.
6 I wouldn't be living in Italy if I hadn't got married to an Italian.
7 I would have phoned you if I hadn't lost the bit of paper with your number on it.
8 If she weren't/wasn't so aggressive, we'd get on (much better).
9 If there's a train strike on Monday, I might not be able to come.
10 We wouldn't have a broken window if you and your friends hadn't been playing football in the back yard.
11 I'd speak to them more often if they weren't so reserved.
12 If I hadn't missed the end of the film, I'd know who the murderer was/is.
13 If Jimmie passes his exams, his father will/is going to buy him a new bike.
14 We'd have gone to the cinema if we hadn't already seen the film
15 Zoe would have won the race if she hadn't tripped and fallen.

6
2 towards 3 on/about 4 for 5 from 6 to 7 to 8 to 9 on
10 in

7   (Model answer)
FUN FOR ALL THE FAMILY AT NEW ADVENTURE PARK
Tamford Towers Adventure Park is set to open its doors to the public this Saturday at noon and, take it from me, it's an opportunity you don't want to miss! The park designers have really pulled out all the stops on this one and come up with what, for my money, is the best adventure park ever! Not only that but also the best value for the money in Dad's pocket with all sorts of special deals and discounts for families on a budget.

Once you're inside, there's something for everyone. There are ten totally new rides ranging from the Water Splash log-ride, which might be a bit tame for some of you teenagers, to the hair-raising 'Screwball' – a type of crazy high-speed spinner – and the awesome 'Abyss', which sends you plummeting to earth at over 100 miles an hour! Totally exhilarating and definitely not one for the faint-hearted!

But there's more yet! There's a small zoo with camels, rhinos and, a must-see for younger kids, penguins! Don't miss their feeding times (11am and 5pm). Then there's 'Uncle Ted's Farmyard', where youngsters can see and even touch chickens, sheep, cuddly lambs and goats. And when they're tired of the animals, there's a large playground with swings, roundabouts and slides. And when Mum and Dad need a break from all the fun, there's a cafe-style restaurant as well as the park's very own pub with beer garden – a popular retreat for fathers in need of refreshment.

And don't forget the souvenir shop (full of marvellous things), refreshment kiosks for ice creams and soft drinks – yes, there are plenty of toilets – and a huge FREE car park! So, don't forget this Saturday – be there or be square!

8

1 after/when   2 state/say/indicate   3 to   4 which   5 where
6 them   7 to   8 of   9 other   10 together   11 lies/is
12 another   13 who   14 along/together   15 out

9

13 ▶ Mind and Body

1

2 … meet outside …   3 by yourself   4 OK   5 themselves
6 … to you   7 OK   8 OK   9 OK   10 … make us …   11 … to each other   12 OK   13 We as …   14 … each of us   15 … to themselves   16 … for each other

2

2 didn't interrupt me when I'm speaking   3 left for the station
4 hadn't lost my temper (this morning)   5 you hadn't/haven't seen her   6 lost your job, what would you do then?   7 hadn't given my number to that insurance agent   8 were poor/broke/didn't have any money!   9 didn't have to go back to work tomorrow   10 hadn't held on to my belt, I'd have

fallen overboard   11 I was somewhere warm and sunny/the weather wasn't so awful   12 were rich, I'd travel round the world in my own plane

3.1

2 insecurity   3 beneficial   4 awareness   5 embarrassment
6 anxiety   7 sincerity   8 resentful   9 dismissive   10 attentive

3.2

12 discontented   13 invulnerable   14 OK   15 dishonest
16 OK   17 OK   18 insincere   19 inattentive   20 unattractive

4

2 sets … apart   3 give up   4 end up   5 clam up   6 shout … down/shut … up   7 carrying out   8 look into   9 face up to

5.1

2 OK   3 shrugged his shoulders   4 clapping my hands
5 stamps his feet   6 OK   7 nodded their heads   8 OK

5.2

9 nail B   10 foot I   11 D heart   12 hand J   13 A teeth   14 E heels   15 H thumbs   16 teeth C   17 eye G   18 F ears

6

2 no matter   3 Much as   4 in spite of   5 While   6 whichever
7 However   8 Despite the fact that   9 whatever   10 However hard

7

2 head-on collision   3 hand signals   4 heart-to-heart talk
5 knee-jerk reaction   6 thumbnail sketch   7 earsplitting noise
8 eye contact   9 blood circulation   10 hair-raising story

premature 2 powerful 3 tightly 4 Protective
unavoidably 6 overheating 7 non-alcoholic
sensitivity 9 childhood 10 artistic 11 painful 12 recovery
importance 14 emotionally 15 consultation

(model answer)

Ms Maria Hempel

I am writing in support of Ms Maria Hempel's application to become a resident health and fitness trainer at your establishment.

I have known Ms Hempel for approximately ten years in her capacity as aerobics instructor at the 'Avalon Club', the gymnasium which I manage.

First and foremost, I would say Ms Hempel is an excellent teacher of aerobics. References to her in our customer feedback forms have been unanimous in their praise for her as a professional. The only slight criticism has been over her modern hairstyle. However, I am sure she would be prepared to adapt her appearance as seems appropriate should she be selected for the post.

Furthermore, Ms Hempel has continued her professional development through a health and nutrition course, which she has just completed successfully, adding another qualification to her portfolio.

Besides her professional qualities, Ms Hempel is also punctual, in excellent health, has a good sense of humour and excellent interpersonal relations with the other members of the instructors' team.

In short, I would highly recommend Ms Hempel as a prospective member of your staff. Should she get the job, it would be a great loss to us here and it will be difficult to replace her.

Jim Long

(15 May 2002)

14 ▶ Testing Times

.1
… you didn't smoke … 3 … you've tasted … 4 OK 5 … I ad been born …

.2
… you'd/had told … 2 OK 3 … relieved if he doesn't come
. 4 … if you hadn't lost … 5 OK

.3
… us playing … 2 … suggested that I spoke/should speak
. 3 … interested in learning … 4 Remember to buy …

5 … try plugging it in?

1.4
1 … it may/might/could be … 2 It can't have been … 3 … he managed to swim … 4 OK 5 … we didn't need to take …

1.5
1 had already been eaten. 2 OK 3 … need testing … 4 OK
5 OK

1.6
1 Despite living/Although he lived … 2 … due to the low …
3 The reason (why) she … 4 … a major cause of …
5 … sport, whereas/while/whilst cricket …

1.7
1 Having lived in the countryside … 2 OK 3 Never having flown before … 4 OK 5 … mother, who lives in Bath, is …

1.8
1 No sooner had we arrived … 2 Not only was the hotel room dirty, … 3 OK 4 What we want is … 5 OK

2.1
2 J running/walking/wandering 3 flying N 4 putting/hiding K 5 to give D 6 to look/appear C 7 to inform H
8 pushing/kicking/shaking/hitting M 9 to tell A 10 I to realise/understand 11 to pay B 12 to think G
13 leaving/dropping out of L 14 being/getting F

2.2
2 being, to get 3 listening, arguing 4 put, paying 5 start revising/to revise 6 participating 7 to be, to get 8 go, taking
9 telling 10 to ban 11 (to) show 12 to run, to bring 13 to leave 14 to make, go

3 (Model answers)
2 Present continuous – I am working in Dublin this month.
3 Present perfect simple – I've already eaten so I'm not hungry, thanks.
4 Present perfect continuous – a I've been waiting for an hour.
b I've been sunbathing in the garden, that's why my face is so red.
5 Past continuous – a I was picking grapes in France this time last week. b I was defrosting the fridge when the phone rang.
6 Past perfect simple – By the time the police arrived, the robbers had already escaped.
7 Past perfect continuous – I had been working for ten hours when I fell asleep exhausted.
8 Future continuous – I'll be relaxing at the seaside this time next month.
9 Future perfect simple – I hope I'll have read her book when I meet her next week.
10 Future perfect continuous – I'll have been working here for three years next June.

4
2 managed 3 were 4 rang 5 leaves 6 miss 7 'll miss 8 'll get 9 's always turning/always turns up 10 arrived 11 to catch 12 had been sitting 13 was going 14 wouldn't

be/wasn't   15 were/was   16 'd catch   17 sails   18 'll have
19 leaves/'ll be leaving   20 was shutting/was going to shut/was
about to shut   21 had just collapsed   22 is still being repaired
23 won't get   24 'll have gone/'ll go   25 get   26 Haven't you
heard   27 came   28 'd listened

5

3 based   4 feedback   5 interviews   6 whole   7 In
8 follow/choose   9 According   10 whereas/while/whilst
11 Moreover/Furthermore/In addition   12 own
13 Strangely/Surprisingly   14 expected/predicted
15 appears/seems   16 addition   17 worryingly   18 felt
19 cause   20 balance   21 However
22 recommended/suggested   23 namely   24 importantly

6

T	I	M	E	L	I	M	I	T	M	T
C	R	N	A	P	C	N	Q	I	F	P
A	B	E	P	R	A	H	U	S	A	R
N	M	R	V	A	K	S	E	K	I	E
D	E	V	G	I	P	S	S	C	L	F
I	O	E	R	U	S	K	T	J	K	O
D	S	S	A	M	W	I	V	E	R	R
A	R	O	D	L	E	A	O	X	T	M
T	Y	T	E	S	T	U	N	N	W	A
E	A	S	T	R	A	T	E	G	Y	N
D	I	N	K	R	I	P	A	N	I	C
O	D	P	A	P	E	R	C	I	Z	E
T	S	I	T	N	G	R	E	L	A	X

7

1 Dolomites   2 adventurous   3 OK   4 quarrelling   5 their
6 panicked   7 dying   8 tried   9 OK   10 paid   11 OK in
American English or travelled   12 extremely

Progress Test Four

1

1 though/if   2 hold   3 to   4 be   5 down   6 at   7 being
8 should   9 to   10 as   11 having/getting
12 clenching/shaking   13 could/would   14 which/that
15 wish

2

1 work out   2 dressed up   3 getting on   4 got away
5 top/fill … up

3

1 Operate/Activate/Set off   2 Attempt   3 extinguish
4 without taking/avoid taking   5 assembly   6 rear of   7
Await (the)   8 collect belongings   9 panicking
10 Remain/Wait   11 told/instructed   12 to re-enter/to return

4

1 it   2 back   3 OK   4 and   5 also   6 What   7 in   8 such
9 OK   10 reading   11 OK   12 situation   13 slowly   14 both
15 written   16 more

5

1 B   2 D   3 C   4 A   5 C   6 D   7 B   8 C   9 A   10 D   11 C
12 D   13 C   14 D   15 C

6

1 personality   2 categorise   3 insecurity   4 generosity
5 inability   6 dismissive   7 unreliable
8 roadworthy   9 solemnity   10 repeatedly   11 unspoken
12 seemingly   13 discouraged   14 nightmarish
15 knowledge